The Luminous Darkness

T0353275

LEIF ZERN

THE LUMINOUS DARKNESS
The Theatre of Jon Fosse

ENGLISH TRANSLATION
BY ANN HENNING JOCELYN

First published in the United Kingdom in 2011 by Oberon Books Ltd
521 Caledonian Road, London N7 9RH
Tel: +44 (0) 20 7607 3637 / Fax: +44 (0) 20 7607 3629
e-mail: info@oberonbooks.com
www.oberonbooks.com

Norwegian edition published by Det Norske Samlaget, Oslo

Published by agreement with Hagen Agency, Oslo

This translation has been published with the financial support of NORLA

A catalogue record for this book is available from the British Library.

PB ISBN: 978-1-84943-058-6
E ISBN: 978-1-78319-264-9

Cover photography: Helge Hansen | www.maneuver.no

CONTENTS

1. ENTRANCE

This book was written by a theatre critic. I have followed Jon Fosse's writing for the theatre since the mid 1990s, a couple of years after his playwright début in Bergen on the Norwegian west coast, not far from the small village, Strandbarm, where he was born in 1959. I had read his novels and was also familiar with his articles on art and literature, later published in a volume called *Gnostic Essays* (1999).

In my native Sweden, Fosse was an obvious point of reference in the young literature written on the bridge spanning the left-wing movement of the 1970s and the post-Modernism of the 1980s. But it was his work for the stage that had me seriously interested, starting with Kai Johnsen's production of *The Child* at the National Theatre in Oslo in 1996. I found it hard to express my response to it, though not because I was struck dumb, the way one can be by certain theatrical experiences. It was more the sensitive, intimate, poetic and secretive quality of this performance – at the same time elusive and disconcerting. It suggested to me that, on the European stage, Jon Fosse's place was that of a stranger.

The Child was like nothing else shown on Swedish and Scandinavian stages at the time. They were dominated by Lars Norén's family dramas and the young British school of the Royal Court Theatre, featuring playwrights such as Sarah Kane, Mark Ravenhill and Rebecca Pritchard. Fosse's play radiated a strange stillness, not to say tenderness, a far cry from the balancing act between despair and irony that so clearly signified the 1990s.

Although the sparse, reduced dialogue of Fosse's language, what's come to be known as 'minimalism', had its own prehistory, this was completely different from Beckett's silences and Pinter's pauses. Beckett's silences are tragic, finalizing the Modernist era initiated by Ibsen and Chekhov that explored, throughout the 20th century, human inner emptiness and yearning to come alive. Aspects of Pinter's dramaturgy – the anonymity of the roles and their obscure pre-history – most likely influenced Fosse's writing at the time of his début, but the same cannot be said for Pinter's interest in social superiority and subordination. Typical of Fosse's characters is their tendency to retreat rather than attack. On the rare occasions when a power struggle occurs in a Fosse play, it is obvious that his preoccupation is with weakness rather than strength.

Still – the closeness to Pinter and his feeling for form should not be denied. Every word has the precision of a note in harmony with the whole, a musical principle more lyrical than prosaic. It's tempting to describe Fosse's later plays as poems for the stage.

A similar language economy is found in the work of the German dramatist Franz Xavier Kroetz, born in 1946 and, next to his better-known compatriot Rainer Werner Fassbinder, a significant exponent of the political theatre of the 1970s. Kroetz' characters, smallholders and 'little people', speak in clichés that reveal them as lacking in both humanity and individuality. Kroetz is Michel Foucault on stage: demonstrating how people are deluded to think of themselves as free when in reality, power speaks through them in a theme of alienation and exclusion.

In Fosse's plays, the impersonal comes across as more hopeful. I know that many people take a different view, but my way into Fosse's theatre seems to have brought me ever closer to the core of his dramatic writing: the mysticism, the fragile balance between emptiness and meaning.

That's not to say that his writing for the stage is without social relevance. As in a developing bath, pale images of a society in crisis emerge: widening gaps between town and country; depopulated rural areas where old people stay behind waiting for children to visit; the feeling of being lost, of belonging nowhere. In the so-called 'information society' each one of us is expected to shape our own identity: Fosse writes with empathy and love about those left behind, those who are neither able nor willing to subscribe to the bliss of self-realisation. Speaking on behalf of the losers, he indicates, more than once, that such loss is not without its rewards.

Reading his work is hard – staging it harder still. He focuses on things that really can't be expressed. If nothing else for that reason, his success has to be regarded as extraordinary. Fosse's plays have been translated into some forty languages and have been performed, since his début in 1993, in nearly nine hundred versions, something of a record for a non-commercial playwright. A young generation of directors have taken an interest in him, and while he has contributed to the development of modern drama, he remains paradoxically solitary, radically impervious to a range of dominant contemporary styles.

I have seen his plays produced in a number of countries. Some of the most sensitive performances have been in French and German. Together with a large number of Norwegian and Swedish productions, many full of insight, just as many poor or simply indifferent, they form the basis of my assessment of his work, just as much as the scripts I've been reading.

The art of drama is an act of interpretation, and the greater the dramatist, the more varied the interpretations. The lack of understanding with which Fosse's work is received in some places is just as remarkable as the recognition afforded him by other directors, actors and critics. He divides opinion into two opposed camps: those who maintain that his plays are too lacking in action to be dramatic and those who take the view that the very lack of action opens the door to an enriched world other than the one routinely explored by the theatre.

It seems to me that most critics agree on the description of his method: for example, that the dramatic action in his plays is sparse, bordering on non-existent. That the action moves around in a circle, returning to the point of departure, ignoring all the turning points of classical drama. That Fosse's plays are difficult to 'grasp'. That there is nothing to grasp in these poetic, atmospheric, often enigmatic texts.

But fragility is not gossamer. Like any original creative dramatist, he writes for a theatre that does not yet exist. It is up to his executors – in whom I include the audience – to dream of realising it one day. He uses an absolute minimum of words to say almost the same thing: *come, go, not, maybe, visit, stay, wait, together, something, disappear, a little, yes, no…* But he gives us these words anew.

Roughly speaking, theatre can be approached in two ways. In one case, you use what's already there: traditions, established methods, knowledge passed down through generations, well-proven to entertain and satisfy the audience. Even clichés are acceptable, as long as they are imbued with new life. Without this heritage, these long-standing skills, the theatre would soon become sterile and, in due course, die out as an art form.

In the other case, a new, radical theatre is built on the ruins of the old, creating the main furrow of modern theatre, with Craig, Artaud, Reinhardt and Meyerhold in the first phase, followed by Brecht, Copeau, Strehler, Peter Brook, Jerzy Grotowski, Peter Stein, Ariane Mnouchkine, Christoph Marthaler and others in phase two; also including of course directors such as Robert Wilson and Robert Lepage, two post-Modernist offshoots of the pioneering spirit of Modernist theatre. A tradition of *tabula rasa* and technical advances.

Fosse can't be said to belong to either of these camps. No matter how much you search for Ibsen and other sources of inspiration in his work – and find them – he still remains an isolated phenomenon in western drama, at once modern and timeless. A leading Fosse director, the Frenchman Claude Régy, has called him the Maeterlinck of our time: a truly significant comparison. The attraction to myth and fable of the Belgian Nobel laureate has no obvious correspondence in Fosse's work, but the ambiance they create is related: ephemeral, often bordering on unspeakable.

Samuel Beckett, Thomas Bernhard, Peter Handke and Elfriede Jelinek – these have all influenced him, though more, perhaps, by offering resistance to inert theatrical convention and blatant awareness than by their way of writing. Bernhard's rages and Jelinek's verbal clusters are the antithesis of Fosse's sparse tonal language. But they do indicate a path beside naturalism, psychology and drama of ideas.

This book deals only to a limited extent with Fosse's other work, which ranges from poetry and children's books, opera libretti and theoretical essays to new versions of classical plays and actual translations. Fosse's adaptation of *Peer Gynt* from Norwegian to New Norwegian was used by Robert Wilson in his version of Ibsen's lyrical drama in Bergen in 2005, and his adaptations of Racine, Sophocles, Goethe and Marivaux are as faithful to the originals as to his own sense of aesthetics.

As a young novelist, Fosse wrote in a Modernist tradition rooted in, amongst others, Virginia Woolf: labyrinths of awareness, with quick interchanges between the external and internal. Remains of this technique can be traced in Fosse's second, rarely performed play *And We Shall Never Part*, perhaps a resonance of the high tempo in his early novels *Red, Black* and *Closed Guitar*. Occasionally, he takes a theme from his prose and adapts it for drama; conversely, an event from a play may turn up in a novel. *Beautiful*, a play from 2001, has obvious similarities to the novel *The Boat-Shed*, written in 1989, while the short story *Aliss in The Fire* (2004) deals with the same subject as the relatively early play *A Summer's Day* (1997), where a woman stands by her window, looking out over the sea, where her husband once disappeared in what was, to all appearances, a suicide.

Jon Fosse can't be divided into the playwright, the poet, the prose writer. If nothing else, there is a strong lyrical streak in all his writing, a musicality that gives his words a magical, conjuring tone, at once simple and intense. A couple of years ago he wrote his first hymn, and it would be surprising if more do not follow. Having said that, something decisive happened at the moment when he decided to write for the stage; as if the theatre liberated something in his own vision; as if the stage itself, with its definite prerequisites of time, space and physical presence supplied the substance of his plays: the elementary conditions that determine human existence on earth.

During the late 1990s and the first half of the 2000s, I saw a large number of Fosse performances in Scandinavia and the rest of Europe, a mere fraction of all the productions he had in this period. If I possessed a magic carpet, I would know more about the way Fosse's drama is performed and received in Albania, Portugal, Iceland, the Netherlands, Poland, Israel, Japan, Brazil, China and many other countries, but the view of a theatre critic is perforce limited by geography.

It happens occasionally that your professional interest is impossible to separate from the personal, and this applies to me in the case of Fosse; I can't think of any other living playwright who speaks to me so directly and makes me face such central issues about the true essence of theatre. It can be argued that the theatre is without 'true essence', but in its moment, every strong theatrical experience carries the stamp of truth.

From personal experience I know that I'm not alone in feeling this. Like few other playwrights, Fosse inspires a special involvement. Today there is a new wave of interest in his work. A growing crowd of directors keep returning to him as to a newly discovered source. Others are more dubious about his claim to greatness. He has not been welcomed by the English theatre with its more realistic compass. When The *Girl on The Sofa* had its world premiere at the Edinburgh Festival in 2002, the director was Thomas Ostermeier, as if a Continental view of Fosse's aesthetic were needed to conquer the hard-to-please home audience.

In Sweden an independent theatre with modest resources, *Teater Giljotin* in Stockholm, was the first to introduce him, while the main stages took only a fleeting interest in this young compatriot of Ibsen. *Dramaten*, the Swedish national stage, home to big names like Ingmar Bergman and Erland Josephson, were remarkably late in performing Fosse and have compensated for this neglect only recently with Gunnel Lindblom's productions of *Girl in a Yellow Raincoat* and *A Summer's Day*. Lindblom, best known internationally as a favourite Bergman actress, was one of Fosse's earliest supporters, directing the world premiere of *A Summer's Day* in Oslo in 1996.

The attitude of the Swedish National Theatre is indicative of Jon Fosse's place beyond the quest for popularity and, in a narrow meaning, topicality. This does not suggest that his plays have nothing to tell our time, but he speaks from a different angle, harder to define than that of most other dramatists.

In the pages that follow, I shall endeavour to chart the way his world is created and his plays are structured; the way they are performed and could possibly be performed. In other words, not so much about Fosse's personal life and background. That he was born in western Norway and writes in New Norwegian is reflected in his returning theme of the sea and the vague yearning for it that besets many of his characters. The shabby old houses stand there, "in need of paint", as it often says in his stage directions. Delicate, like living beings, they call out for someone to take them in hand and care for them.

New Norwegian is more than a Norwegian dialect, it is now one of two official Norwegian written languages, created in the mid 1800s as a reaction to the national tongue much influenced by Danish. There is a rich literary tradition in New Norwegian, to which Fosse belongs. The slow music of ocean waves can be heard in his dialogue:

> Now we've come to our house
> Our house
> where we shall be together
> You and I alone
> in the house

where you and I shall be
alone together
Far away from the others
The house where we shall be together
alone
with each other

Even though I'm convinced that both the seven-year-old and the teenager from Strandbarm are still present in each line and each setting of each play and its language, their expression calls for an explanation other than biographical. And even though international interest in Fosse is coloured by a certain exoticism, his success on the world stage can't be referred to any form of 'primitivity'. To focus on Fosse's background and upbringing would be to gravely underestimate both his general awareness and his modernity.

I find that I'm hardly ever reminded of other playwrights when I see his plays on stage. Instead I tend to think about my own life, about existential issues, about the essence of time, this basic chord of everything he touches, and most surprisingly, of other art forms, such as music and film, directors like Carl Dreyer, Robert Bresson, Roberto Rossellini and Yasujiro Ozu, the Japanese master. This is not to say that Fosse strives to emulate them or to translate their aesthetic into his own expressions. Naturally, my associations in an encounter with Fosse's work need not be his. Rather, I would say that ideas in a wider sense, philosophical as well as religious, occupy a significant position in his writing. They are determined by a vision or thinking that can't be incorporated within the limits of any genre or tradition.

Theatre is to a large extent bound by its own rules, and part of Fosse's greatness is his consistency in breaking these rules, whether aesthetic or social. In order to properly understand him, it may be necessary to momentarily forget the stage and instead look in a different direction.

2. FROM PAGE TO STAGE

For Fosse, the road to the theatre was never open in the way it is for many other young people approaching the stage. He was not one of those who are born into the business. At the time of his début with *And We Shall Never Part* in Bergen in 1994, few people would have thought of him as a future dramatist, and I believe he himself shared those doubts. You only have to read his early essays to get a clear picture of an author more drawn to literary theory. Fosse had been studying philosophers such as Bakhtin, Benjamin, Adorno, Heidegger and Derrida. His writing was definitely exclusive. If the 1970s had been the decade of the theatre, the 1980s were again a decade of literary fiction. The theatre had been swift in following the political winds during and after the 1968 student rebellion. Any art that wasn't socially applicable had been quarantined. Co-operating with, amongst others, contemporary novelist Jan Kjærstad, Fosse raised a challenge to this view: literature, they contended, is answerable to no one but itself.

Since it can be read, drama certainly is a form of literature, but it is a literature awaiting the language of body and action. Even the silences of Beckett's late plays contain the sound of someone breathing and looking for words. "Translating for the stage is translating the spoken word", wrote the influential Swedish critic and director Göran O. Eriksson in a comment to one of his Shakespeare translations. Writing for the stage certainly has the same aim: a dramatist must be prepared to have his lines coloured by the actors speaking them, no pure stage language exists.

On the other hand, a concept like 'spoken language' is best avoided in terms of theatre, since it suggests colloquial language.

Stage language is essentially different, neither colloquial nor purely literary, but more a liberation from both, inviting a view of ourselves as hypothetical figures taking part in an experiment. A good example of this is *The Tempest*, where Shakespeare has placed Prospero and the other characters on an isolated island, exposing them in a new and sharper light.

In Fosse's dramatic work, the language issue is pushed to the limit: in his essays he gives, typically for the 1980s, an account of the background to his writing, what he himself calls the 'voice of the text'. One of his main points of departure was Mikhail Bakhtin's idea that the novel is a polyphonic communication, where the author allows room for several voices: no single narrator can lay a claim to the whole truth; it takes a multitude of voices to make up the living, unfinished context. Similarly significant was the concept of irony of Schlegel and the Romanticists, seeing irony, not as 'sarcasm' but the insight that a text is constantly generating new meaning. It's an irony different from the colloquial language irony, expressed through saying one thing and meaning something else, all the time with a subject controlling the act of speech. In a written text this subject is missing. Still, meaning is created or, in Fosse's own words: "Meaning is a miracle."

So what brought him finally to the theatre?

The material he had already produced – novels, children's books, poetry – contained hardly anything to suggest that he was harbouring manuscripts for plays which, a few years later, would be among the most advanced, vividly discussed to appear in the theatre in our part of the world. His successes were so striking that they soon attracted special attention. He wasn't merely 'Fosse' – he was referred to as 'the Fosse phenomenon', and critics like me who followed his spectacular progress on European stages were often asked how this phenomenon could be 'explained' – as if he were an alien just arrived from another planet.

All important art appears surprising when first introduced. But this one was somewhat enigmatic. Did he belong amongst us?

Fosse himself has talked in various contexts about his hatred of the theatre: he never wanted to go there, and possibly, it was this hatred that finally made him a playwright. In an essay he writes of his view of dramatic art and the wall of alienation which kept him away from it for a long time. "I'm a playwright, but honestly, that was never my wish. On the contrary, I didn't like the theatre and have said on various occasions, for example in interviews, that I really hated it, at least the Norwegian theatre."

The director Kai Johnsen, an early advocate of Fosse's art, writes in a survey of Norwegian drama of the 1900s about a 'war' between playwrights and Norwegian theatres. Few theatres would collaborate with playwrights: one of those affected was Terje Vesaas who, like Fosse, wrote in New Norwegian. Possibly, coincidence could have brought Fosse the same way. However, this Norwegian civil war was a special case of a more general manifestation: Fosse's 'hatred of the theatre' represents a deep-rooted tradition, a shadow that has haunted the theatre throughout its history, from its origins in the ancient world to the present obsession with new forms of communication (swift, digital, barrier-pushing). In the 1990s, the debate of 'the death of the theatre' was rekindled once more. While it's rare to hear talk of hatred of film or literature away from strictly Puritanical circles, hatred of the theatre is a living tradition.

The French theatre scholar Georges Banu differentiates between two types of theatre hatred: external and internal. The external type is the one expressed by Plato, the Fathers of the Church and medieval bishops: to them the theatre, for good reasons, was a threat to their own doctrine. Would people go to mass or to see the players? Plato, as is well known, wished to banish poets from his republic and took a similarly jaundiced view of actors. On a stage anything could happen. Was that not the very antithesis of the principles of philosophy: predictability, constancy, eternal truth?

The Church's time-honoured hatred of the theatre is easy to understand. More interesting is the fact that this tradition lives on well into our time amongst intellectuals, who see the theatre as an art form inferior to, above all, literature. The concept of autonomy pertaining to classical Modernism is incompatible with the fundamental impurity of the theatre. Amongst typical theatre-haters I find the Swedish poet, critic and Modernist Artur Lundkvist, for years from 1968 onwards an influential member of the Swedish Academy. Lundkvist considered film to be a modern art form – the surrealist Bunuel! – while the theatre, with its outmoded technique, stumbled along behind it.

Banu's point is that the view of theatre as unworthy compared to other art forms is just as common amongst theatre people themselves. Stanislavsky, Craig, Meyerhold, Artaud, Grotowski, Kantor, Brook and Wilson all dreamt of a plague, a purifying purgatory or at least a radical overthrow that would kill the theatre and lead to a rebirth. Unlike Plato and the moralists, they didn't want to banish the theatre: they wanted to *save* it.

If the external hatred of the theatre focuses on its very *existence*, the internal type rather attacks its *condition*, and this is where I believe the young Fosse belonged: fully doubting the theatre's ability to remain free of the compromises and commercialism imposed by its dependence on approval by a fickle audience. In his book *The Empty Space*, Peter Brook writes about the 'deadly' theatre. Aware of that affliction, Jon Fosse kept himself at a safe distance from it.

As a young man, Augustine, Father of the Church, had dreams of becoming an actor. After his conversion, in *City of God*, he wrote some of the best known lines against the theatre, stating that, while an ordinary plague affects a person's body, a theatrical performance is a plague that will destroy his character.

For amusement, one can look upon Jon Fosse as a latter-day Augustine, though active in the opposite direction. From his highly literary point of departure, he viewed the art of theatre as a less worthy form of expression. Reluctantly, he let himself be persuaded to write a play for the National Theatre in Bergen. The rest is theatre history: some thirty plays written in almost two decades, countless productions all over the world, an inevitable presence conquered by the strength of his vision. Like all important playwrights, he has changed our understanding of theatre itself.

In other words, a convert?

Yes and no. To me, Jon Fosse never ceases to be an Augustine in the world of theatre. In nearly everything he writes for the stage, there is an unmistakable quality of distance, a hint of doubt that can't be ignored, a little seed of distrust remaining in his plays like a paradoxical promise. His hatred of the theatre may be only a small detail in his background, but it is not insignificant. He came to the theatre as an alien, and such a one he remains.

3. THE CONTEMPORARY STAGE

At the time when Fosse wrote his first plays, the Soviet Union had collapsed and several countries in its projected shadow had taken their first steps from dictatorship to freedom. But the Balkan war soon turned utopia into dystopia. Conflicts of a kind that most of us would have associated with the past broke out in our own back yard: a senseless slaughter using culture, language, religion and history as their sharpest weapons, finding its enemies, not on the other side of the iron curtain, but in neighbours' houses, where toys were torn from children's hands while their mothers and sisters were raped. These were tragedies evoking memories of the Crystal Night and the pogroms of the 1930s: tearing apart old concepts, they introduced new ones in the political vocabulary: ethnicity, violence, terrorism, xenophobia.

Europe, it would appear, had become more liberated but also less secure, all of it in a paradoxical atmosphere of inebriation and hangover.

But it wasn't just the revolutionary year of 1989 and the Balkan war that released this slide in the social and mental landscape. In the UK, Margaret Thatcher's Conservative government in a short time had achieved a fundamental transformation of society: the distant war was reflected in the inner lack of security of a system where two opposite poles faced and boosted each other. The rest of Europe was not excluded, but in England the effect of social changes was noticed both earlier and more clearly than in other places.

British theatre was not late in reacting to these new conditions. There was a dammed-up need to regain some of the social prestige that drama had enjoyed with the 'angry young men' of the 1950s and their successors in the 1970s. Many dreamt of a repetition of the effect caused by John Osborne's *Look Back in Anger* at the world premiere in London in 1956, and they soon had their prayers heard: the 1990s finally got its socially engaged drama. Jimmy Porter in Osborne's play rages against the British Establishment. His brothers- and sisters-in-arms forty years later live in a borderless Europe.

This is what the set is like when Fosse enters the stage: a world full of blood, violence and social disintegration.

Two of the most interesting and emblematic plays of this epoch deal with the double exile – internal and external – eating into the European social body during these years: Sarah Kane's *Blasted* and Lars Norén's *Romanians*. Kane's play takes place in a Leeds hotel room, where a rape at the beginning of the piece is repeated and escalated when a soldier from the Balkan war blasts the walls of the realistic room and in the final part violates the first violator, as if the one transgression imitates and provokes another, in an endless chain of atrocities and contempt of life and human dignity.

Norén's play does not contain as much external violence and didn't give rise to the same inflamed debate as Kane's explosive piece. But his description of the Janus face of exile has obvious similarities to hers. A man and a woman, Romanian refugees, are in a New York hotel room, a symbol of the vacuum where their future will be determined. In the following scene they visit a considerably younger couple living in a basement room nearby: two lean, isolated and, by all appearances, disturbed young people on the run from parents, school and society. The connection between the first couple and the second remains obscure. They meet by chance. What we see, nevertheless, are two states of being echoing each other. Both the youngsters and the refugees are victims of the disintegration that, like the effect of an earthquake, seems to spread over the entire developed world.

In Lars Norén's play, civil society has been transformed into a war zone. Kane's play, placed next to this picture, is a parallel exercise. When Bosnia moves into a Leeds hotel room, it is already there, as if Europe's interior and borders had been redrawn and exile had become common territory.

At the Royal Court Theatre in London, within the course of a few seasons, a generation of dramatists emerged who were seen by critics as a more or less homogenous group: Rebecca Pritchard, Mark Ravenhill, Nick Grosso, Joe Penhall and Jez Butterworth, to name a handful of these grandchildren of Jimmy Porter. They were called, amongst other things, 'the new brutalists' and wrote in such a way as to hit the audience head-on – what came to be called 'in-yer-face'.

Sarah Kane's play caused a scandal and hit the headlines. Even the corps of critics had divided opinions about the value of showing social degradation so directly and nakedly on stage. According to Benedict Nightingale, the typical play of the 1990s is a big city drama where young criminals dump their enemies in plastic bags and drugged boy prostitutes are serially raped, as if it were the most natural thing in the world. Dramatic development and conflicts in the classical sense of the word are given a low rating in this fisticuffs theatre; they are replaced by situations, provocations and frightening momentary pictures.

There was such a shift in the drama written in the 1990s, from inner dynamics to external, from dramatics to visuals, from being enacted to being demonstrated. With aids like film, screens and video, the realistic violence could penetrate even further on to the area occupied by the stage. Sarah Kane's plays were compared to the films of Quentin Tarantino, an analogy she herself refused to subscribe to: her despair is free of every form of sensationalism.

Onstage violence is of course to some extent always sensational, dramatic and upsetting. It makes us close our eyes or stare. Western theatre, from Sophocles and Shakespeare to Edward Bond and Sarah Kane, can thus be described as an anthropology of violence, the study of the role of violence in the human world. The ritual roots of theatre testify to such a connection. Today, with audiences inured by daily war scenes on television, stage violence needs to be intensified to elicit a strong emotional reaction. But the question is, where do you draw a reasonable line between *portraying* violence and giving it *dramatic application*?

In other words: what happens to a drama that is more intent on *showing* something than *enacting* it in terms of conflict or dilemma?

When it comes to Fosse's work, the question, as usual, has to be reversed: how far can you go avoiding a concrete external course of events without ending up stultified and undramatic?

The British model was not the only one around. On the European continent there were other, more transcendent forms of stagecraft. Dance, inspired by Pina Bausch, gave the theatre a welcome push in a less literary direction, and one of the most highly esteemed directors of the period, the Swiss Christoph Marthaler, in a playful search for a theatre that could overturn the existing concepts and sabotage audience prejudice from inside, made an obvious connection to the anarchist dadaism of the 1920s: a form of deconstruction, not academic but generous and full of loving nonsense.

At the same time, the workshop method of the Royal Court in London spread to the rest of Europe. In 1999 in Berlin, Thomas Ostermeier became Artistic Director of the Schaubühne, Peter Stein's prestigious theatre. He himself directed several of the most emblematic plays of the young school, from Sarah Kane's *Crave* and David Harrower's *Knives in Hens* to Mark Ravenhill's *Shopping and Fucking*, plus – a contribution to the dystopian diagnosis of society – Lars Norén's *Personal Circle 1:3*.

As part of this chapter, Ostermeier also took on *The Name* by Fosse in a driven but not entirely unproblematic production, where contemporary irony took over a family portrait, making it a shade too dystopian, more akin to the way other playwrights of Fosse's generation would treat a similar theme: as if it weren't possible to imagine a modern sitting-room without giving it an ironic kick in the groin. The production wasn't bad – on the contrary, the performance had a nice edge to it – but for that very reason it challenged the consistency of Fosse's dramaturgy. While Ostermeier saw clearly the uneventfulness of Fosse's play, its avoidance of conflicts and turning-points, he couldn't resist reflecting the unspoken part through the typical ironic view of the 1990s, as if the absence of violence merely concealed the real thing. The over-dimensioned room, the ugly fashion in clothes and home décor, the intrusive sense of alienation and rural 'retardation' – all these effects contributed to undermining the tenderness for people and things that is Fosse's distinctive mark.

Of course we all laughed at the mother obsessed with cleaning and at the slow-witted father stumbling on the threshold each time he went into the kitchen – but were they really worth laughing at? I don't believe the essence of *The Name* can be so easily caught in a style or in a tacky environment. What was lacking in Ostermeier's version was something nameless and unguarded, beyond the theatrical need of social diagnoses and psychological explanations. *The Name* got sorted under a label belonging to the Schaubühne of the 1990s.

Fosse's plays have often been hijacked by contemporary trends, made supernatural or performed with heightened irony. This can easily be explained by his reluctance to follow the rules of classical dramaturgy when it comes to handling crises. Some directors give an impression that they want to save Fosse from his own mistakes, as if the slowness and the repetitions of his dialogue were children's diseases that will go away eventually. Such an approach is bound to fail.

In order to capture his distinctive art, you need a gentler term, like intangible. That does not mean inaccessible, on the contrary. In reality he comes very close to us, close enough to make us lose the control and insight we thought we had, leaving us at a loss for words.

4. THE ABC OF WAITING

In Fosse's first plays, the characters give an impression of being on the run away from the world of other people. Never at home, always on the way somewhere. In *And We Shall Never Part*, a woman walks around her flat waiting for a man who, by all appearances, has left her. When, surprisingly, he enters and makes it understood that "he's had a hard day", one gets a fleeting impression that there is a world out there, with a normal weekly rhythm of work, leisure and rest. Dinner is on the table, as in any realistic play. But this impression quickly fades when the man and woman go on talking to each other across an abyss of time and space and he suddenly disappears again. Are they married or divorced? Is it her reminiscing or is it all happening in the present?

Just as vague is the location in *Someone Will Arrive*, where a man and a woman have sought refuge in an old house by the sea, where nature seems to prevail over environment:

> And imagine when there's a storm
> when the wind
> blows through the walls
> when you hear the sea pounding
> and the waves grow higher
> when the sea is black and white
> imagine how cold the house
> with the wind blowing through the walls
> and imagine how far away other people
> how dark it is
> how silent it will be
> and imagine the wind blowing
> the waves pounding
> imagine what it will be like in the autumn

in the dark
with the rain and the dark
A sea in black and white
and only you and me
in this house
so far from other people

They travel here in order, he says, to be alone together,
something she doubts is possible.

But is that possible
Won't the others
still be here
Is it possible to leave all the others
Is it not dangerous

Before long, they are visited by a neighbour: he turns out to
be the man who sold them the house. His appearance means
that the woman's premonition will come true: they are not alone
here either, there is always a village nearby, it is not possible
to protect symbiotic love from rivalry and jealousy by isolating
yourself in a social vacuum. No human dwelling is empty. If
nothing else, we are caught up, sooner or later, by fantasies and
memories.

This is one of Fosse's recurring themes: characters placed in
the flow of time, unable to defend themselves against either the
past or the future. Precisely what we are trying to avoid becomes
our destiny, as happens to the man and woman who bought a
house in *Someone Will Arrive*. They believe they have found a
place beyond time and space – a non-place, a favourite word
in Fosse's vocabulary – but are made to observe this nameless
location invaded by what has been and what may come. Just
as the house has a history, every living thing has a future, the
present is mainly a fiction, a fragile shield against the waves
coming from two directions, eating themselves into its shores.

If Fosse's characters appear shadowy, that's because they can't avoid thoughts of *what may happen*. The possible is always more real than the actual. Above all, in his early plays this notion is a threat to security – later it becomes a utopian illusion. That is why Fosse keeps writing about upheavals: changing your flat, buying a house, escaping and returning, as if each new location could offer what the past did not.

Each line is a wing-beat between two moments: in the middle of the line, contradictions undermine the experience of a *present* existing in the characters' life, a fixed point in time when we are at our truest to ourselves:

> I have never been alone
> I have always been alone
> I have never not been alone

These lines are uttered by the lonely, abandoned woman in *And We Shall Never Part* – smiling, she looks at the man who, according to the stage directions "*is not there*", and then she lies down "*as if her head was on his lap*", addressing in seductive, caressing terms his absent character:

> And you must have missed your girl
> She's not bad, is she
> And you have missed your girl
> I know that
> *She raises her hand, as if caressing his*
> *cheek, smiles towards him*
> My lovely boy
> I've missed you

In the next moment the man enters the kitchen, saying: "But I'm here now". Happily, she replies: "Yes, you're here now" – before, just as suddenly and for no apparent reason, she goes to the window, turns round again and continues her monologue, now "*in despair*":

> He can't just leave
> He has to come back
> He can't just leave
> He'll soon be back now
> He can't just leave me like that
> I miss him so

How are these bewildering lines to be understood? Is the man there at all, or is his visible presence on stage just a figment of the abandoned woman's imagination? Is the play her waking dream? And the man the one she dreams of? For the spectator the conclusion is near at hand when the man at the centre of the drama enters in the company of a younger woman – 'The Girl', as she is called in the list of characters – who seems to have taken the place of the first woman and is now preparing to move into the flat. We hear the voices of the man and the girl from the passage outside the room while the woman is still on stage. The girl hesitates, unsure whether she has a right to be there. "I'll leave if you don't come".

So far the entire arrangement, with its fluid demarcation between dream and reality, could be a drama of jealousy, with the first woman the conscious part of the play and the others 'actors' on her own inner stage: the man who has gone off with another woman, her musings seeking comfort and then resignation, all in a single flow of daydreaming and fragmentary reminiscing, with people disappearing, reappearing, disappearing again, as if all phases in this extended process were coming together at precisely the moment we witness: before, now, later, in a flowing continuum.

Reading this into the play, the woman becomes both the main character and its subject: an eye seeing on our behalf, as lonely at the beginning as at the end, when she turns once more to the still empty end of the sofa, smiling and saying tenderly:

> Are you there
> *Pause. She smiles broadly*
> Yes there you are
> Of course you're there
> You're there now

But the play is more original than that, for even if it seems to be about visions taking concrete shape on stage, it's only partly a dream play where the actors are fantasies in the head of the dreamer, free to walk, with theatrical logic, through walls and ages.

Fosse has never been a stranger to the modern dream-play tradition, started by the late Strindberg and the symbolists around Lugné-Poë at the Théâtre de l'Oeuvre in Paris in the 1890s, with Ibsen, Maeterlinck, Hauptmann and Claudel as resident playwrights. When the living and the dead interlace their lines in Fosse's *Death Variations*, it's easy to presume that this was his aim all the time: a dissolution of time and space allowing him to write for a theatre that, in Strindberg's famous foreword to *A Dreamplay*, strives to "imitate the incoherent but apparently logical form of dreams". Fosse himself encourages such a suspicion by calling one of his plays *Dream of Autumn*, a masterpiece, in several regards seemingly following Strindberg's dictum: "Time and space do not exist; on an insignificant reality base imagination spills out to weave new patterns: a blend of memories, experiences, free associations, absurdities and improvisations."

But however fluid his definitions of time, Fosse is no usual writer of dream plays. The concept of a dream play should in any case be handled with caution. Having been applied far too often, it has lost its precision. In Strindberg's Buddhist-coloured philosophy, there is always someone dreaming our lives and keeping us in the dream until we awaken ("one consciousness above all others, that of the dreamer"). Fosse has a similar Gnostic idea of captivity and possible awakening, but in his case there is no sign of the gap between dream and reality that took off post-Strindberg, leading straight into the standard repertoire of modern drama.

In Shakespeare's plays, everyone wakes up sooner or later after a stay in the irresponsible kingdom of dreams: "I have had a dream, past the wit of man to tell what it was", says Bottom the Weaver in *A Midsummer Night's Dream*. Demetrius, one of the young people in love, expresses the same feeling when he rises drowsily from the confusion. "Are you sure that we are awake? It seems to me that yet we sleep, we dream."

Shakespeare's interest in dreams can be explained by the fact that he lived in an era that saw the modern self come to life and experience its first crisis. How are we to know that we are awake and not dreaming? His plays are full of questions about the evidence of the senses. Sight and hearing are fragile sources of knowledge, as Hermia becomes aware:

> Methinks I see these things with parted eye
> When everything seems double

There is something alluring about her double vision, as if the stay in darkness and unconsciousness could heighten the feeling of being alive. Hermia wakes up to something new. She goes from darkness to light, and the same applies to the spectator who sees a successful production of *A Midsummer Night's Dream* – you leave the theatre feeling there is a future, just as a sense of peace and possibilities can be evoked by Strindberg's *A Dream Play*.

In Fosse's plays, there is no such dynamic. The statement that 'life is a dream' has lost its magic. He is more obsessed with sleep than death. His characters are frequently in a state of sleep or fatigue, as if life and death were all the same.

Early on, sleep becomes a *leitmotif* in Fosse's drama: the sister of death.

But let's return to the abandoned woman in *And We Shall Never Part* to examine her role in the drama. It's a fact that the play begins and ends with her monologues, rendering the reality status of the man and the girl less certain. If they are mere walk-ons in her consciousness, the action assumes a 'normal' chronology: she is in the *present* of the action, fantasising about events *before* and possible *events* later.

However, if we penetrate the overriding structure of the text, another, more interesting pattern emerges: the first woman is not the only one here waiting for someone else. The insight we ought to pick up is that all three of them are waiting for each other in this no man's land between being at home and leaving, between saying goodbye and returning. They are all equally scared of being abandoned, equally unsure of their place on the rotating axis of time and space.

Who in this drama is really waiting for whom?

The man accusingly tells the girl that he has driven on slippery roads in "rain and slush", walked "up and down streets" and "banged on her door" just to see her. All the time she has, he fears, been with another man. If the first woman is jealous and 'waiting', the man could literally steal her lines – and does: "I waited for hours" he tells the girl, adding:

> You were with him
> when you came at last
> I came to you and you were with him
> *In despair*
> Why do you have to
> be with him

The literal meaning of this line is that we can never forget, just as we can never leave behind what we have been. The past sticks to the girl when she is first heard in the wing: "I'm a bit frightened." In the same way, the man and woman still live on in each other after separating, and this restlessness, these fluctuations between absence and presence are reproduced in their world, eating into the present and further into their future. They are all repeating each other's lines. Before long, the girl, too, falls into the ABC of waiting:

> I didn't think you'd come
> I thought
> it was just something you said
> that you just said you'd come
> I didn't think you would

Now, if not before, we have to give up the idea that the abandoned woman is the subject of the play. *And We Shall Never Part* is not a drama about her jealousy, loneliness and comforting invocations. Although the role is a monologue, it flows into the others to form a common voice. Listen to the play's lacework of lines:

> He has to be here soon
> - - -
> You didn't come
> - - -
> He mustn't come
> - - -
> I always miss you
> - - -
> What is there worth waiting for
> - - -
> Now you may come
> - - -
> You have to wait for me
> - - -
> I can wait
> - - -
> So come then

Who is speaking here? All three! Their lines echo each other. A is waiting for B, who is waiting for C, who is waiting for B, who is waiting for… The knowledge, like a musical theme, emerging from this series without a beginning or an end, is formulated one final time in what has to be seen as the key phrase of the play: "Life is all waiting".

> People sit in their rooms
> They sit in their houses
> in their rooms
> they sit there waiting
> amongst their things
> secure in amongst their things
> they sit there waiting
> in the houses under the sky
> sit there waiting
> in the rooms
> in the houses
> amongst their things
> they live waiting
> and then they don't wait any more
> And the things remain

This could be a motto of all Fosse's writing for the stage, from his début to later pieces such as *Sleep* and *I Am The Wind*. If there is a main character in *And We Shall Never Part*, it's not the lonely woman but time itself. *And life is waiting*. Not so much waiting for something concrete as the existential phenomenon of waiting. Life is basically nothing but waiting, being suspended between the past and the future, in a present that cannot be captured.

"So come then" – The Girl's last line as she stands hidden behind the door to the corridor – thus becomes a line in condensed form revealing time and space to be running parallel in Fosse's world. She is doing the same as everyone else in this piece: waiting. On the threshold of something else.

5. COMING AND GOING

It is often said that Fosse is a dramatist of stillness and silence. This is both true and not true, for while his characters remain still and silent, passive and inactive, they give an impression of constantly being on the way to somewhere. Contained in the stillness is a restless unease. Each pause lives on its opposite. The man and woman in *Someone Will Arrive* have hardly entered their house before you sense that they will move away from it. They talk feverishly about the vacuum and the refuge from others that they are seeking in this place. Only the wind and the waves will be heard. Even so they fill the silence with their anxious talk.

They are not only *here* – they are, above all, *not there*.

If Fosse's early plays led away from the immediate vicinity of people, the two that followed – *The Name* and *The Child* – represent a journey back to more inhabited areas, and also to a more traditional genre: the realistic family drama, with an ordered chronology and action pointing forward, not going round in a circle.

But this isn't done unconditionally, for even if Fosse doesn't shy away from accepted forms of drama, he tends to stop in his tracks when he gets too close. This is obvious in *The Name* with its family constellation and lack-lustre rendering of two young people about to set up home together. *Nightsongs*, which came three years later, lacks neither a specific setting nor typical contemporary markers (suburb, triviality and vague future prospects). But beneath, or above the one drama, another one emerges, as in double exposure. Fosse's settings are only partly social, more like some borderland: existential, mental rather than physical, with something ending and something else beginning, and where, sooner or later, everyone has to choose whether to stay behind or move on.

Just as vital as the role of time is to understanding Fosse's dramatic work are his descriptions of the scenic space: to see a Fosse play is always seeing someone rushing past, as if the only task of the stage was to render this passage visible. There are plenty of doors and thresholds in Fosse's plays, and his dialogue follows the same pattern. "Well I suppose I had better leave" – or, with contrapuntal effect: "Don't go".

The Name, Fosse's third play, nevertheless contains an obvious attempt to distance himself from a dramaturgy risking to emerge as too abstract. An elderly couple are visited by their pregnant daughter. In the list of characters she is called The Girl but her name is mentioned as Beate, perhaps in contrast to the nameless He, She, The Man and The Girl in his earlier plays. The parents live on the outskirts of a small village near the sea. Fosse likes to denote his locations as beside, outside or in transitional zones.

The play begins with Beate sitting alone on the sofa of the sitting-room waiting for the others: her mother and father, a younger sister who still lives at home (an elder sister has left) and her boyfriend, who lets her take the bus while he himself will follow in his car, suggesting a precarious relationship. Close to her time, Beate suspects that her boyfriend is embarrassed and does not like to be seen with her. When he knocks on the door it's a while before she opens. It turns out that he had nearly got lost.

> I didn't find the house
> *Brief pause*
> And when I finally
> found it
> and knocked on the door
> no one came to open

The girl here is in every sense of the word *at home*, unlike the unfamiliar surroundings in *Someone Will Arrive*, where strangers had lived in the house. The girl is one of many returning characters in Fosse's world. But she doesn't visit very often, as emerges from the mother's comment: "I haven't seen you for a long time" and the typical echo of the father's statement: "It's a long time since she was here".

In *The Name*, the house, the family and the village form concentric circles, and even if the house in Fosse fashion is situated near the sea, in shelter behind a hill, the village is close enough for the mother to go shopping there, with a crutch to support her, as she has a sore foot. The social environment, so conspicuously absent in Fosse's earlier plays, has now drawn closer: each entrance brings with it something of the world out there: the father's job, old school-friends. "So this is where you grew up", the boyfriend says to Beate after glancing at the surroundings, and soon the mother arrives, bringing bags of shopping and gossip. "Guess what I heard down at the shop". Almost like a television soap with a high factor of recognition.

Here, on the border between town and country, a simple triviality reigns, which ought to astonish everyone confronted with the sense of escape in Fosse's earlier work. On one wall is a wedding photograph giving the boyfriend an idea of the family before he knew them and that may be why Beate has come here: because she is expecting and felt an impulse to return to her origins, although it's done without any relish. The following scenes are undramatic. The father comes back, tired and hungry after a long day at work and at first takes no notice of Beate's boyfriend. Instead the mother chats away to fill the silence, while the sister gets excited and, like all little sisters, wants to feel Beate's bulging stomach. The only worrying thing is the sister's mention of a young local man called Bjarne, which gives rise to a suspicion that it may be he and not the boyfriend who is the father of the child.

The subject is not explored further but is an example of the pathology of jealousy that makes the men in Fosse's plays so restless. Upheaval is often connected with separation and divorce. Though I'm not convinced that his characters depart because they separate: it's more as if they separate in order to depart. Behind it all is their basic unease.

So – on her way to give birth and set up home, Beate pays a rare visit to her parents. Even so she's hardly across the threshold before she regrets it. The feeling arises at the moment she recognizes the sitting-room and discovers the objects in her childhood home. When her boyfriend makes a tentative effort to say something approving she replies:

> I don't want to be here
> I'm ill at ease being here

Why? The answer, of course, is a truism: because she'd rather be somewhere else.

All places are temporary refuges. This applies to the person departing and to the person returning: no one stays in one place for long.

Those who have followed Fosse's development as a dramatist will sense that this is the kind of life and environment that the man and the woman seek to escape from in *Someone Will Arrive*: neighbours, routines, recurrences that can be broken only by new and temporary upheavals. It's a fundamental theme:

> I don't want to live here
> I don't want to be here

The young man aspiring to be a writer who takes his own life in *Nightsongs*, the son studying literature at university who seeks out his mother in *Mother and Child*, the old woman waiting for her husband in *A Summer's Day*, the daughters who shut themselves in their rooms in *Visits* and *Death Variations* – it is tempting to make a jigsaw puzzle of these parents, children, siblings and lovers who, adding one annual ring to another, make the Fosse tree grow, age and shed its leaves. One likes to think that they are the same people returning later in life. That they form a family, joined together by destinies and enriched experiences.

But there are no such connections in Fosse's dramatic work, no biographies or destinies, and anyone expecting Beate and her parents to enter the stage to tell who they *are* have gone to see the wrong play. Fosse's characters are not interesting in that way – rather, they are anonymous, interchangeable, impersonal. They all wear a mask that could represent anyone open to an identification different from the expected. They often use the pronoun 'I' but could just as well say 'you'.

Ostermeier's production of *The Name* contained a scene which jarred more blatantly than the others. When Beate and her boyfriend discuss the name of the expected child they come up with different suggestions, most of which are rejected. She writes down all the boys' names to the left on a piece of paper and all the girls' names to the right, while he fantasises, he says, about "the unborn children", their curiosity about being born and finally coming to their earthly parents.

> Well I've been thinking
> that there is a place where children
> live together before they are born
> where children are in their souls
> But they still talk to each other
> in their own way
> in their own angelic language
> *The boy looks at the girl, smiles*
> And as they think ponder
> where they might end up
> For they don't decide that themselves
> And then it's decided where they will go
> One child after another
> will be decided for

I'm going to Norway
one child says

The boyfriend sums up his philosophy on life saying, in order to be human you must think of mankind "as all the dead and unborn and all those who live now". Beate agrees with him that that's a nice thought and suggests that they take a walk so that he can "feel the wind". With a laugh she adds that it may bring on labour. At the same moment the little room they are in is extended, assuming a place in a wider era connecting the names of the dead to those of the living in a space without beginning and end.

In Ostermeier's version it was hard to see how this change of scene could be incorporated in the rest of the performance, as it couldn't be explained in terms of psychology. The sudden seriousness of the boyfriend inevitably came across as misplaced in Ostermeier's lightly ironic portrait of the ridiculous family. There was no place in it for the speech about the unborn children.

Young people who get a place to live, expect children, miscarry, give birth, visit their parents, break up – events like these constantly occur in Fosse's plays and appear in new combinations. The same simple words are repeated: "And then we can go and see the old house where you grew up."

However, in the middle of this triviality, as in an X-ray, both clearly and enigmatically, the skeleton of another person appears: someone standing by the window watching the rain, opening the door, leaving and returning, remaining silent, becoming engrossed in a book, lying down on a bed... all in a constant fluctuation between presence and absence, where life at every moment takes place on the borderline between the two, which is where we are.

Take note of the negations filling Fosse's dialogue with distance and fresh upheavals. I believe the most common word in his plays is 'not', and the favourite verbs of his language are not 'be' and 'have' but 'come' and 'go', using synonyms like 'part', 'leave' and 'die'.

I didn't find the house

These are the boy's first words when he arrives at the girl's home and knocks at the door. Here, on the threshold of this unfamiliar room, Fosse's theatre begins. Let's open the door and enter.

6. IN THE BEGINNING WAS THE HOUSE

A couple come walking across a yard, a middle-aged man and a younger woman. They approach a house, turn the corner, stop to watch the house, of which they are the new owners. They are about to move in, take possession. But the man procrastinates before producing the key to insert it in the lock. They linger outside, walk along the side of the house, look out over the sea, sit down on a decrepit bench leaning against the wall of the house, all reasons to put off the decisive moment.

She is the one uttering the first line of this early Fosse play: "Now we'll soon be in our own house." Even so they hesitate on the threshold of the new, beset by fear and misgivings. Anything said from now on sounds at once reassuring and disconcerting. It is repeated so persistently that you suspect they themselves doubt that their dream will be realised.

> Not alone
> But alone together
> *She looks at his face*
> Our house
> In this house we'll be together
> you and I
> Alone together

In play after play, Fosse's characters approach a house like this. As we've seen, *The Name* begins with the boy knocking on the door of Beate's parents' house and entering when no one answers. His entrance is followed by several others: first the sister, then the mother, the father and, finally, Bjarne. Step by step the spectator is brought into the house. The boy, says one stage direction, "*walks around a little looking at things in the*

45

room". He's familiarizing himself with the setting, studying the photographs on the sideboard and on the wall, asking after the others, then "*goes to the window, looks out*".

The front door opens and the sister enters. The mother returns from her visit in the village and shakes the boy's hand before "*slowly turning round*", then disappears out through the kitchen door "*closing the door behind her*". The father comes home from work, pretends not to see the boy, sits down, reads a paper, takes a few steps on the floor and looks out of the window before "*going into the kitchen, closing the* door *behind him*".

In the same way, the description of the girl's entrance in *And We Shall Never Part* contains a complete choreography:

> He looks towards the kitchen door, then looks towards the front door, sees The Girl enter, she is in her mid-twenties, her hair is long and wet, she closes the door. He looks again towards the kitchen door. The Girl stands watching him". Shortly thereafter comes this wide-angle movement: "The Girl gets up, then walks on to the floor, keeping both arms close to the body, stretches them out, then looks at the ceiling, lets her eye move around the room. Then she goes to the window, stands up to look out. She quickly turns to him.

Amongst theatre directors it's common practice to go straight to the dialogue, ignoring the stage directions, which are seen as a more or less deliberate attempt by the playwright to direct his own play, or at least control its interpretation. The often pedantic stage directions of naturalist plays got a bad name after Ibsen and Shaw. Modern designers are not interested in furnishing rooms. Since Peter Brook, there has been a prevalence of either the empty space aesthetic or multi-medial fantasies opening up other worlds. However, when working with Fosse's texts such an approach would be a fatal error. His entrances and exits are much more than stage directions: they are the notes of his music and should be read as indications of tempo or chords added to the actors' lines. The rhythm of the phrases is heard in between them.

It's always said about Fosse that the decisive moments occur in the spaces between the lines, in the unspoken words, in the mute movements forming a language of their own beside or just beneath the sparse dialogue. But it's not a rule. In *The Name*, as we have seen, the boyfriend says little in the first part but much more in the next as he elaborates on the unborn children. For each silent character in Fosse's plays there is usually one who can't keep his mouth shut. Often, this is the same person.

Personally, I believe that this fixation with Fosse's pauses can only be explained by the way modern theatre has essentially allied itself with psychology. Each text is assumed to have a subtext carrying the truth of anything the text does not disclose. In *The Name* we have a tendency to interpret the boyfriend's reticence as diffidence or embarrassment, a sign of something he'd rather not reveal. The circumstances could be seen as awkward: a young man visiting his future in-laws for the first time, with a possible reason to presume he's not welcome. But on what do we base that assumption? The dialogue gives no firm indication in that direction, and even if it were true, it doesn't have to mean that the circumstances are dramatic. They could just as well be undramatic.

Our problem with Fosse's pauses probably says more about the attitude we bring to the theatre, expecting that both the loquacious and the silent characters have something to hide, that each line and each pause is a symptom of something else, a veil closing around the role, which the actor and, finally, also the audience, are commissioned to remove. In other words, the 'reticence' of the boyfriend would need a diagnosis before it can tell us something. An anchor somewhere in his emotions, his psyche, his past. A message addressing who he is and, above all, how he *became* who he is. When Beate's curious sister asks him what he's going to be, he replies: "Nothing".

Suppose that he's telling the truth, that this is all he has to say. Why do we find it so difficult to accept that idea?

Freud and psychoanalysis are behind most acting methods in modern Western theatre, such as practiced by Stanislavsky, The Actors Studio and their more or less faithful followers. You learn to handle your inner conflicts by talking, by not keeping silent. This gave rise to the notion of the spoken word as the opposite of silence. He who talks is willing to communicate, he who does not speak, consequently, has something to hide, as if each pause – and there are plenty of those in Fosse's plays – were a gap, an accident of language. We have long lived in a culture of candour and confession. He who stays silent arouses suspicion and makes us look for the hidden truth. Fosse teaches us something else: that we don't have to search, that it's pointless, not because his characters are without feelings or harbour difficult experiences, but because the truth of our lives expresses itself in different, less tangible ways.

Watching Fosse on stage is like entering a room. His characters are, physically, our guides. They cross the threshold, enter or exit, open a door, close it carefully behind them, go to a window, look out, turn round – on principle never resting, though they rarely achieve anything. Beate's parents lead a monotonous, uneventful life, the mother leaning on her crutch, the father with his apparently tiring job. In the midst of this uneventful life, they are constantly stirring, incessantly busy making a move: the mother intruding and retreating, the father getting up from his easy-chair, leaving through the kitchen door or just "turning round to look out of the window". Therefore, the audience has to be prepared to see these plays. To experience them as visual events in the room. Yes, more than that: you have to see the dialogue shaped as part of the choreography, the characters speaking, thinking aloud, staying silent and with their lines crossing the same thresholds in an extension of time and place. The past and the future change places, as do inside and outside. The one who opens a door becomes visible or invisible, takes a step from another room, past a vague fleeting present, heading into the future.

For Fosse, the stage is not just the place where something happens: at the same time it is the event. Someone entering or exiting, steps being heard and disappearing, are linguistic events leading us into the physical progress of the play. Silence and speech are two sides of the same coin. A pause is not a gap in the dialogue. If so, we might as well call the word a gap in the silence. For this reason there is nothing mystical about Beate's boyfriend being both silent and eloquent. His pauses hide nothing, they just follow his speech the way one word follows another. There is no hierarchy between different kinds of signage in Fosse's dramas: silence is not a deviation from non-silence. The door that has opened has a visible and invisible side to the audience, but it's the same door, and the one passing through it is the same person.

In his novel *Melancholia*, an extensive work in two volumes published in 1995 and 1999, Fosse describes how the Norwegian painter Lars Hertervig, in 1853, sits in the basement of Malkasten in Düsseldorf, where he is an art student, remembering how his father took him to a Quaker meeting in Stakland, Skjold:

> And I and my father walk off along the shore, stepping on the pebbles, then there is a path up a steep slope and my father and I walk up the path, first my father, then myself, walking a few metres behind him, and my father stops, he takes off his cap, rubs the sweat off his forehead with the sleeve of his jacket, breathes heavily in and out, says it's heavy to walk in this heat and we still have some way to go before we are there, we have to walk up from the lake to the road, then along the road for a bit and then we'll come to the little house in Stakland, a small house it is, built jointly by the Quakers of Skjold, but it isn't a church, for Quakers don't want to have a church, no, it's a simple house, as simple as can be, a room, a window, and in the middle of the room, chairs in a circle on the floor and when we arrive, when we enter the room, I shall just go and sit on a chair and then sit there quite still not speaking, trying not to think, and any thought that appears, the minute it appears, I am to try hard

to banish, make it go away, anything worrying or anything to please me I shall try to banish, so that only small pieces remain, turning into nothing, or almost nothing, for then it will be silent inside me, there will be a silence inside me and in that silence I can find peace deep inside myself somewhere and then, if I'm in grace, I may be filled with a cool light, not of heat but a cool light, so shimmering, so heavy and at once so light, so overwhelming, that I have never before seen a light like it.

Lars Hertervig's recollection houses the complete set of a possible Fosse play: a house, a room, some chairs and nothing else, as if the 'someone' crossing the threshold into this room were to step straight on to the stage. As we know, Quakers allow for both speech and silence. Those sitting down here abandon themselves to time, waiting for something to happen. There is a clear connection between Fosse's preoccupation with the Quakers' ideology and the basic chord of his own theatre. In an interview he has talked about the role Quakers played in his life during an early period in his life. Fosse has revealed that it was his grandfather, a Communist and Quaker, who introduced him to their tenets:

> Quakers have no priests, no rituals. They sit in a circle when they meet, say nothing – unless someone feels like talking. What's significant for both Quaker weddings and funerals is stillness. Quakers believe that man has something of God inside. The unique part of each individual is connected with God. Silence removes worry and confusion and brings you close to God or the light inside yourself. In good literature that is what I like – the silence.

In Fosse's world people are silent, not because they lack words. There is not the slightest gap between speech and silence, only this threshold – as between two rooms – passing from one moment to the next: time and space interlaced on stage.

7. A PRINCE WITHOUT A SWORD

At an early stage, the label *minimalism* was attached to Fosse's dramatic writing, not without good reason: the sparse dialogue, the repetitions and the remote landscape in several of his plays suggested the image of a playwright searching for something simple and reduced, in contrast to the documentary directness and barrier-pushing multitude favoured by many artists of his generation. He himself has mentioned in various contexts that he accepts the concept of minimalism as a description of his writing for the stage. However, I don't think this should be regarded as submission to a concept of style.

Fosse's minimalism, it seems to me, has two faces. On the one hand, a critical dissociation from the contemporary media-orientated artistic stage that gives equal status to high and low, blunting the audience's attention in competition with the loud demands on topicality typical of advertising and popular culture. On the other hand, an affirmation of the inner way of silence and mysticism, an active search for a lateral position, a reluctance to involve himself with contemporary issues.

Finally, conclusively, this ambivalence can be seen as two sides of the same coin. Perhaps there is in fact in Fosse's plays a decisive tension between a pronounced protest against the noise of media and a seclusion going its own way: a tension between criticism and detachment.

The problem with the concept of minimalism is its versatility. It is a rather vague generic term for a number of styles within, above all, architecture, painting and music, all having their roots in the post-Modernism of the 1960s. It would certainly be both possible and rewarding to compare Fosse's sparse dialogue with the music of Steve Reich or Arvo Pärt, the meandering conundrums of the former and the sacral monotony of the latter: ideal for our present-day non-confessional religiosity. It can't be denied that there is an affinity between Fosse's preference for the small format and the kind of prudence that invites meditation and trance-like states. In *Someone Will Arrive*, just a few lines are repeated and varied, getting their power from the prophecy already established in the title of the play. We see two individuals caught up in a fixed idea, at once painful and alluring. There is a captivating attraction in this maelstrom of compulsive thoughts repeated so often they are finally verified. Everything revolves around this point of a needle, like the dance of a shaman.

Fosse's minimalism is not a matter of style. The fact that so many persist in seeing it as such says more about our confusion when it comes to interpreting his plays than about the actual happenings on stage. I like to think that his light shines into the darkness: into our lack of certainty and orientation, not unlike the sentiments expressed by his characters.

Early on, the casts contain only few characters. They are nameless, called He, She and The Man in *Someone Will Arrive* and He, She and The Girl in *And We Shall Never Part*. But, as in cell partition, the original triad grows into a larger group. The claustrophobic mood of jealousy gives room to a wider field of dependencies. The next step is a family, either about to be formed – as in *The Name* – or already a fact – as in *The Child*, where the main characters meet in the first scene, live together expecting a baby in the second, and finally, are struck by tragedy in the third, when the baby is born prematurely and dies. All of a sudden, Fosse is so close to the classical family drama that one could suspect him of wanting to convince those doubting him that he, too, can write 'proper plays'. In *The Name* the young man visits his girlfriend's home. In *The Child* it is the girl's mother who intrudes with presents, bags of food and meddlesome though harmless comments.

And I'm so looking forward to becoming a grandmother

I just wanted to look in

No I'd better be going

We'll be in touch

The three following plays – *Mother and Child*, *The Son* and *Nightsongs* – revolve around similar family-related themes, with a constantly repeated feature of children visiting their parents or parents making unannounced visits to their children. It always happens over wide distances in time and space and, as a remnant of the unease sweeping through the empty, sparsely populated rooms of the early plays, there is a feeling of upheaval, as if each place of abode were only makeshift. The man and woman in *The Child* – their names are Agnes and Fredrik – happened to meet late at night at a bus shelter; now, having moved into their home, they are already talking of finding something else:

And we can move
We don't have to stay here
We've moved so much in life
both you and I
We don't have to stay here

Though trivial, this is a highly significant Fosse line, suggesting something of the homelessness adhering to a word like 'home'.

Some time later, Agnes and Fredrik have moved from the suburb to a house by the sea. In the last scene of the play they enter the church they visited when they first met at the bus shelter. At the hospital, while Agnes is examined by the doctor, Fredrik has a long conversation with a nurse, who tells him she is childless and, like him, comes from a place by the sea. They both long to go back ("Yes we must be close to the sea"), and in these apparently disparate scenes – a meeting at a bus shelter and a conversation in a hospital waiting room – three Fosse themes converge into one: the child, the sea and faith in God:

> Water and sea
> Living water
> as they say

Concretely, it's about the child that Agnes and Fredrik miss and mourn, the coastal landscape that they want to return to, the church they visit at the beginning and the end of the play. These three themes return and merge in the long conversation between Fredrik and the nurse. To his question, whether she intends to train as a midwife, she replies: "I suppose that was my intention." Jon Fosse the poet is no warm advocate of metaphors and symbols, but here the thought of the sea and amniotic fluid is clearly anchored in the image of a budding midwife.

The Child is a key text in Fosse's dramatic writing. From there you can trace almost anything he has subsequently written for the stage. People go on moving house, changing flats. The young parents in *Nightsongs* have recently moved in together and are visited by the man's mother and father. It's a reflection of the generation gap when children come home to their parents and the same parents later in life visit their children to see their grandchildren. You can therefore talk of two events of equal importance in *The Child*: while Agnes and Fredrik are waiting to become parents, her mother dreams of becoming a grandmother, one reflects the other and, typically for Fosse, refutes the feeling that the present weighs more heavily than the past and future. The passage of time matters more than the moment, which is no more than a chimera.

Now his plays are more often about children and parents, with one significant addition: grandparents. It is rare that a meeting between a child and a parent is described without the child's life horizon being framed by yet another generation.

Already by introducing the theme of the unborn children in *The Name*, those who live elsewhere, just waiting to arrive here – the author has approached the idea of life as a continuation of the present and the past. Beate is ill at ease in her parents' home and doesn't know why she's there: "I can't stand being here". It only reminds her of what has been. "It's all coming back". Exactly what we're not told. It's her childhood as such that haunts her when she goes around looking at photographs of herself. "I certainly wasn't a pretty child". The mother's empty chatter is enough for Beate to lose patience and reply ironically, though it's not so much a conflict with the parents as an experience of meaninglessness.

> Weren't you going to tell us something
> Something you heard in the shop
> Something that made you laugh

In amidst this nameless unease, Fosse opens the door to something else: when, in the next scene, the parents-to-be discuss the name of their child – Kristina after her grandmother or Olav after his grandfather – the main focus shifts from the nuclear to the extended family. The experience of here and now is filled by the knowledge that the self is no more than a shard in the great crucible of time. The play takes a step from the psychological and social theme to one existential and religious (and by religious I mean not so much faith in God as the sense that there is something greater than man, a different chronology, an added dimension).

The family pattern returns in Fosse's fifth play, *Mother and Child*, where the child is a son who visits his mother after a long time. Judging by appearances, she lives on her own and has been upwardly mobile, going from modest childhood conditions in the Norwegian West Country to the civil service in Oslo. The son has studied philosophy and literature abroad. She left him early and also left his father, just as she also left the place where she was born to go out into the world. Against the son's vague future plans Fosse sets the mother's ruthless ambition. She is a bureaucrat, he an intellectual reading Yeats, Joyce and Beckett. She brags about her rise from grassroots to real power, a female Peer Gynt, riding a billy-goat to the land of the future:

> From fjord and mountain
> right to the centre of power
> or at least
> almost
> to the centre of power

This geographical metaphor – *from the West Country to Oslo* – reflects modern social development, from neighbourhood to global networks. For a Fosse play we are told quite a lot about the background and social position of the characters. You see before you a piece of a map of Norway. The concept of *place* is a central one for Fosse, though not by name or history of the place. Therefore, words like Oslo and bureaucrat appear almost brutal when they are spoken in *Mother and Child* – normally, biographical and geographical details are completely absent in Fosse's plays, in contrast to the focus on identity that's the poison of our time.

So far, *Mother and Child* could be seen as an exception in his body of work. It has a clearer division of light and darkness than *Someone Will Arrive* and *The Name*, where conflicts were vague, bordering on imagined. Beate's unease, as we saw, was not better explained. Being born is enough to experience your mother as embarrassing. In Beate's case the feeling of disaster is biological, not social, and her pregnancy the reason for her anxiety.

In *Mother and Child*, the point of departure is biological as well as social. One is reminded that Fosse studied sociology at university. The play contains a kind of social analysis, revealing an unexpected side to this playwright. It is a miniature drama about a mother who makes a mockery of motherhood. She has abandoned her child for the sake of self-realisation at any cost. Her whole life is described as a delayed teenage rebellion, aimed at the Puritanism of her childhood and her own mother's naïve faith in Jesus. As a child, she tells us, she wasn't allowed "one single thought of her own"; and definitely not dancing, playing cards or letting her hair down. Her career is a revenge on an oppressive childhood environment and, at the same time, a project of emancipation; she does not hesitate to call herself a feminist and does not shy away from the idea of reaching the top of her profession, even though, coquettishly, she denies it.

At one level, *Mother and Child* can be interpreted as a variation of the fable about someone who 'wins the world but loses her soul'. Our female Peer Gynt squanders her inheritance and ends up on her own, which is the price she has to pay for her individualism; she is a product of the Norwegian welfare society, that is, successful, and already well on the way to betraying its fundamental values.

At the same time, this tale of success emerges as a crime against nature. The son believes that his mother wanted to have an abortion and was prevented by his father. When she vanished from their life, he moved in with his maternal grandmother, who provided the warmth and affection refused by his own mother.

As so often, Fosse connects the generations. With simple images of Jesus and the land of Canaan, the grandmother was able to transfer strength to her grandson, faith without theology. Keeping to Fosse's conception of the world, one could say that it was this grandmother who delivered her grandson and saved his life, while his mother aborted him after the event, physically with her absence, emotionally with her coldness.

In *Mother and Child,* we hear one of Fosse's most dramatic dialogues, full of turning-points of a kind that rarely appear in his level flow of lines. To begin with, the mother is unsure and tentative, replying to the boy's monosyllabic Yes and No with an eloquence suggesting a guilty conscience. Later she retreats and before long, a certain role-playing emerges in this micro-level power drama: contrary to expectation – after all, he is the one who should be on the offensive – she takes the initiative and speaks ironically about the great difference between his interests and hers, indicating with false modesty the contrast between her own life as a hard-working professional woman and his refined occupation with 'major issues'.

> I don't think too much
> any more
> of life and death
> and all those things
> I'm content

She soon goes further than that, pushing her breasts out, asking whether they aren't as lovely now as when he was little and loved lying on them, as if her son were an escort she wants to impress, even seduce. It's a somewhat incestuous game, making us wonder who is the adult here. If there is a given order between children and parents, it seems to have been suspended. That she would be attracted to him – or attempt to attract him – may not be the most challenging part of this cat-and-mouse game. It's the lack of seriousness: what we witness is the collapse of an order. When she asks him if he is homosexual (since he hasn't found himself "a sweet little girl"), the dialogue takes yet another step into the quagmire that forms the theme of this play. His reply that he is a "sexual sadist" at first makes her appalled, then delighted. "That sounds exciting". The game is driven to a perilous point.

Therefore, he ought to stop it. Speak clearly. Put a spanner in the works. Go from words to action. Instead he shies away and evades her provocations. A couple of ironic retorts – like the line about being a sadist – are rather defensive and self-ironic, another confirmation of his inhibited aggression. If he reminds us of anyone it's Hamlet in Gertrude's bed chamber, but he is a prince without a sword, and this gives her an advantage he is unable to challenge. The question we finally ask is – would he want to? Is he, like Hamlet, prepared to hold up "a glass where you may see the inmost part of thee", as Shakespeare writes – or does his visit aim at something else?

Finally she poses the question: "Tell me what you were doing in Oslo", to which he gives his exit line: "I came to visit you." It's hardly an answer, neither she nor the audience get the answer they've been waiting for. His voice is heard fading out from the passage between the sittingroom and the front door. That's all.

The most remarkable and most effective thing happening in Fosse's drama is what does *not* happen there. We see a story unravel between two parties. Formally, this looks like the classical definition of a conflict in a tragedy: two characters so distant from each other that a compromise is excluded. But Fosse turns form inside out. As in a chorus, the son repeats that he hasn't come to take his mother to task. "No I don't hate you". Not even the knowledge that he was an unwanted child makes this potential avenger a Hamlet in the modern, successful Oslo of the 1990s.

> But you left me with Grandma
> and with Dad
> when she was too frail
> to have me living
> with her
> You just left
> No I'm not accusing you
> even if it sounds that way
> don't misunderstand me
> But

Listening carefully, one can hear a pendulum here, between a 'not' and a 'but', between reproach and acceptance. The rest of the dialogue is full of the same retreats, so vague, it's tempting to interpret his "I'm not accusing you" as a confirmation to the contrary. It sounds like a fear to express what he's genuinely thinking. But that conclusion is not backed up by the lines. There is no 'genuine' in Fosse's dialogues, only ambiguity, a half-expression vacillating between two emotional levels. Anything else would be a violation of the feeling of loss and retreat they express. A conflict would awaken the ego, force it to go from ambivalence to action. But this is exactly what does not occur.

The tension in Fosse's dramas develops along different routes, and I believe that one of these leads to, or originates in, the central role played by generations in his portrayals of families. One could say that the presence of a grandfather or grandmother loosens the tight knot of connections tying a child, for better and for worse, to its parents. Just as in real life it's a kind of 'relief'. Somebody else is there to take over. You're liberated from yourself.

Despite the darkness in *Mother and Child*, a sunlit glade emerges each time the son's maternal grandparents are mentioned. They not only saved the life of their grandson, they provide Fosse with a chance to de-dramatise the rigid pattern of conflict we expect in the constellation of mother-and-child. In a landscape inhabited by Fosse's stray nameless allies, we see human beings branching off back and forth in time, each a link in a chain, with the presence of something greater making us lost, melancholy and uncertain.

Ibsen's inveterate liar Hjalmar Ekdal would be meaningless without the truth-teller Gregers Werle. Hamlet cannot be imagined without Claudius. Tartuffe needs his Orgon, as Orgon needs Tartuffe: on the one hand a trickster, on the other one who needs to be tricked. They define each other. Creon against Antigone: the interest of the state against the eternal laws of the gods. Dionysus against Pentheus: the transformation of inebriation against rational control.

This is more or less the favourite scenario of Western drama, and in his famous analysis of *Antigone*, Hegel maintains that tragedy is achieved when two equally heavy arguments do not allow for compromise. It's impossible to get close to Fosse without accepting that he does not subscribe to such a view. A more even weight falls on his characters. They are not set *against* each other but stand side by side. Using a concept applied by the French literary scholar Georges Poulet to Marcel Proust's *In Search of Lost Time*, the method could be termed juxtaposition. Awareness of the world allows for no hierarchies. Nothing above or below. No basic dichotomy.

Does this mean that Fosse's plays are not dramatic? Certainly not – he manages to create drama of uncertainty itself, the lack of clear alternatives, the painful edge where we face the same question as in the quotation by Dante, used by him as a motto for *And We Shall Never Part*:

> I didn't die, and I wasn't alive.
> Think for yourself if you have a little sense,
> how I was when I was free of both.

The tension is less about conflicts between living beings than the inherent conflicts of living. The feeling of homelessness and alienation. Time splitting us up into our former selves and the future rushing towards us, making it feasible to talk of ourselves as not dead and not living.

8. THE DEAD MOTHER

Are Fosse's characters happy or unhappy? Do they suffer or do they only appear to be suffering?

The questioning may appear naïve. You expect the characters in a drama to be tragic or full of conflict or – as in Shakespeare's and Shaw's comedies, the most classic of all – facing difficult obstacles that they have to overcome, from lovers' tiffs to marriage. Happy and unhappy characters belong more to the world of the novel, as in the case of Tolstoy, Austen, Flaubert and the Brontë sisters, as to the modern reader, who weeps and suffers with the characters in the books.

But in Fosse's plays, the naiveté of the question assumes an obvious relevance. He takes a special interest in elementary issues, those shunned by literature and painting as being too banal and uncomplicated. His texts are rarely about conflict and transformation, but about feelings and mental states, so vague that the characters themselves can't tell what issues they face as they turn to each other. The son in *Mother and Child* is one of these typical Fosse characters.

> No I don't hate you
> Or perhaps I do hate you
> and so I hate all women
> No I don't hate you
> I just
> If I hate someone
> it's not you
> but
> yes
> perhaps
> perhaps I hate
> No I don't know

In the middle of his speech he vacillates between two points of view without settling on either. This really is an impossible speech. Three 'perhaps' in twelve lines. The effect is not like the pointed stance of two parties in a drama pushing their arguments, driving them to the edge. With Fosse, the words echo each other. "But I intend to kill myself anyway", the son says early on in the play – the mother's echo comes later, like a wave rolling back and forth.

> I should have killed myself
> Long ago
> I might as well kill myself

Suddenly they change places, or rather – compete for the *same* place. The initial conflict becomes relative. We become unsure of their motives when one party steals the theme of the other. What remains is a fundamental ambivalence. In spite of her persistence and his awkwardness, both seem to give way. If he is lacking in self-esteem, it turns out that she suffers from the same:

> I tell you
> But you won't believe it
> that I like you more
> than I like myself
> Just so you know
> If it were my life
> or yours
> you're welcome to mine

Suddenly, her substantial ego has shrunk to the size of his. As usual with Fosse, they revolve around the same spot. Truth and falsehood fluctuate as they give and retract, doubt and pluck up courage, say nothing or let the words flow. In that sense, the conclusion is just as perplexing for the audience. What happens to his hatred? The thought of suicide is brought to mind. "But I intend to kill myself anyway", he says, smiling. That line, too, carries a significant ambivalence. Is he serious when he says he wouldn't mind dying?

"I came to visit you", he says when he is already leaving.

Was that all?

The passive stance of several Fosse characters is so complete, it's akin to depression. The young man in *Nightsongs* dreams of a future as an author. He spends his days on the sofa, never goes out and entrenches himself in his flat, as in a prison. His script is rejected by one publisher after another. Although he's just become a father he seems unable to shoulder the weight of that responsibility. At the end of the play he shoots himself. "He shot himself", as one character says. I find it hard to believe that Fosse did not have the curtain line in Chekhov's *The Seagull* in mind when he formulated this echo of Dorn's laconic statement in Chekhov's play: "The fact is, Konstantin Gavrilovich has shot himself."

But when Chekhov's young author dreams of a drama that will one day awaken mankind, Fosse's nameless main character is free of any such revolutionary or Modernist notion. He doesn't have the strength to get up from his lethargic slumber on the sofa, and rather than battle with his indifferent surroundings, he gives up, takes a gun and puts an end to himself.

Sleeping and resting are passive states recurring regularly in Fosse's work. In *Someone Will Arrive*, the jealous man curls up on the bed and speaks into the wall. A person who submits to fatigue rejects initiative, resolution and success.

The French psychoanalyst Elisabeth Roudinesco, in her book *Que'est que la psychanalyse?*, writes that nowadays, mental suffering manifests itself in depression. The symptoms show a strange mixture of apathy, sadness, passivity and search for identity, where not least the latter appears paradoxical, considering that the sufferer rarely acknowledges the value of some kind of self-expression: the freedom afforded by our modern society is so complete, it can't be applied. People expect immediate gratification and become depressed when they fail. New and old therapies are tried and rejected in a flood of salvation theories and lifestyles promising freedom without liberation, progress without history, well-being without loss: a dangerous illusion feeding the very monsters we battle against.

Depression, not unlike a diluted form of the old melancholy, has become the epidemic of our modern society, in the same way as hysteria was the predominant diagnosis in the Paris and Vienna of the late 1800s, with Jean-Martin Charcot in the Salpétrière hospital and in Josef Breuer's well-known analysis of Anna O. The modern individual no longer recognizes resistance as a path to freedom and maturity. The main concept of psychoanalysis is immersed in medical treatment and happy-pills taking away the suffering without calling into question its meaning.

According to Elisabeth Roudinesco, the avoidance of conflict characterizes the era of depression: we resist unhappiness instead of seeking to identify the reasons behind it. This only leads to more unhappiness. Her analysis is confirmed by the high level of anti-depressants prescribed today. Sufferers are becoming younger and more afflicted. Fatigue, burn-out and indeterminate feelings of boredom and meaninglessness are diagnoses that were largely unknown fifty years ago. Today the popular press is full of them, drawing our attention, like an old-fashioned medical handbook, to just how sick we are: I'm not well – thus I exist.

In one of his books, La Fatigue d'etre soi, the French sociologist Alain Ehrenberg manages to capture the essence of this epidemic, that is, 'being tired of yourself', tired of being 'who you are'. If Roudinesco defines depression as the death of the ego – an ego no longer born in conflict with internal and external forces – Ehrenberg states that depression as a diagnosis is encouraged in a society where old-fashioned notions of duty, guilt and discipline are on the way out. The norms of our time emphasize personal initiative and individual responsibility for happiness and unhappiness. Depression succeeds when conflict fails. We look upon mental suffering in terms of inadequacy and deficiency rather than an expression of internal conflicts.

One of Freud's best known competitors, Pierre Janet, a French doctor and psychologist, had a theory of nervous debility (psychasthenia, neurasthenia) as a cause of mental illness. A hundred years later, our western lifestyle experts have revived this long-since discarded diagnosis.

These descriptions have obvious similarities to certain conditions in Fosse's plays: fatigue, erosion of the ego, boredom, fear of conflict. If the young indecisive characters in *The Name, Mother and Child, The Son, Visits* and *Nightsongs* had been in therapy, they would have been told that, not only do they lack ambition and future prospects – that's what their parents' generation would have said – but also that they have to make choices and single-handedly, as it is said, 'construct' an identity of their own. Become somebody. An advert would have added: get themselves a life.

The suicide in *Nightsongs* is followed the same year by another, in the beautiful play *A Summer's Day*, where an old woman stands by the window in her house looking out over the sea where her husband disappeared once while out fishing. It is never verbally confirmed that he took his own life but it's the conclusion the audience draws after hearing him in retrospect talk about his anxiety and his longing. When the woman asks him if he no longer likes being with her, he replies:

> It's not that
> But it's so silent here
> It's so quiet
> it makes me uneasy
> to be here
> I might say
> *He laughs a little*
> Oh I don't know

The theme of suicide is varied in *Death Variations*, where a young girl leaves life on earth without either her parents or the audience understanding why. A vague longing and unease push her over the edge. While Lars Norén's characters want to kill each other, a Freudian theme, Fosse's characters dwell on the thought of killing themselves. They have no enemies. It's the march of our society from neurosis to depression.

In Western theatre, King Oedipus is one of the original myths. In his wake follow a long row of patricides. The point is, murder can take place in the imagination. According to the myth, every son wishes to kill his father in order to take his place. All theatre in this Oedipus tradition is about inheriting; the eternal mimesis of Western drama. Hamlet has to take his father's place, Osvald takes over Captain Alving's illness, James Tyrone Jr submits to James Tyrone Sr – this fateful imitation and rivalry were inherited by the sons of Arthur Miller, Tennessee Williams, Sam Shepard and Lars Norén: they all want to stick a knife in their father, whether in fantasy or reality.

Fosse's sons in a startling way break the logic of this myth. In his plays it's not a question of killing a father but living in the shadow of *the dead mother*. Her absence rules the characters' lives. In *Mother and Child*, the pattern emerges in the portrayal of a mother who mocks her own motherhood and seems keen to seduce her son. The father, who is only mentioned, appears to have been present in the son's life and is referred to as "kind", but he has never filled the place that ought to have been his. That is why the Oedipean dynamic is missing in Fosse's plays. The rebellion is absent.

The dead mother? I take that concept from the Egyptian-born French psychoanalyst André Green, who refers to *la mère morte* to describe a feeling of complete emptiness, not the defeat of the ego to a powerful superego but a kind of passive obliteration, a depression not 'black', but a white, smooth, colourless lack of everything. Green points out that he is not talking about the 'actual death' of the mother but about a mother who is dead in her child's eyes.

I find it hard not to see Fosse as a portrayer of the depressive society. In his plays from the mid 1990s, a white light of negations extinguish all aspirations and dreams of a future.

> You're lying there reading
> You don't go out
> You do nothing
> We have no money
> You have no work
> We have
> nothing

The object of these accusations is the young man lying on the sofa in *Nightsongs*, perhaps the darkest of all Fosse's plays. The brief visit by his parents – they take the first bus back home again – strengthens the impression of total isolation, silence and meaninglessness. The physical confinement points in the same direction. The man's only occupation is to walk from the sofa to the window and the pram. The woman makes an attempt to leave. But she is unable to make up her mind; he has, as she says, "always been kind to me", in the sense given to the word kind in all these plays: a normal state, an absence of guilt excluding feelings of both revenge and retaliation.

As the title suggests, this is a nocturne, a dark, melancholic piece singing the characters to death and rest. If I suggest that one could, or even should, relate to psychoanalysts such as Elisabeth Roudinesco and André Green in order to understand and interpret the depressive moods in Fosse's plays, it's not because I am primarily interested in psychoanalysis – Fosse hardly lends himself to psychoanalytical readings of the classical Freudian type. But I can think of few modern thinkers who have managed to describe, with the precision of Roudinesco, Green and Ehrenberg, the transition from one society to another, caught by Fosse with his images of passive non-subjective weak egos. According to Roudinesco, the loss of subjectivity is the disease of our time. The notion of the ego permanently in conflict with forces in the unconscious has been rejected by the contemporary world of ideas and been replaced by the idea of the depressive personality. Whoever can't imagine a different existence may as well be dead. In consequence, people are tempted to come alive with the help of drugs, New Age, religion, or a health and body cult.

Fosse's characters are unable to say 'I' without adding a negation. Even so it's not enough to see their passivity as a symptom of the depressive society; that would be simplistic. I don't believe for a moment that Fosse ever intended to criticize or even describe conditions in the so-called post-industrial achievement society. He is not that kind of an author. It's true that his characters live within the bounds of that society – but not necessarily on its terms. Beate's boyfriend, when asked what he's going to be, replies, laconically and perhaps reluctantly: "Nothing." It's hard to determine whether this apparent lifelessness fits the diagnosis or if it's resistance on his part. Happy or unhappy? There is an ambivalence which I believe is the main dynamic in everything Fosse writes for the stage. Listening to this "Nothing", could certainly have you worried, but it can also, paradoxically, suggest a feeling of freedom. Something tells me that it's possible to turn your back on your own ego. There is another way to exist.

The man in A Summer's Day may have taken his life. But it would be superficial to suggest that this was merely due to depression. "I'm quite happy too", he says without irony to his wife, continuing: "It's not that". In that case, what is it? He can't explain it, no more than explain why he enjoys spending so many hours alone in his boat at sea:

Well it may be boring
I don't know
But I like it

This "I don't know" contains the same obscurely radical gesture as that of the boyfriend's "Nothing" in the earlier play. They are two answers that refute the validity of the question and leave it wide-open. We have to focus on what he says, not try to interpret it. *I don't know.* The woman by the window doesn't know either. And yet she stays there all the time. We see two versions of her: young and old, and in this double perspective, in these exchanges between then and now, a narrow passage opens up between the past and the future, the very structure of the piece giving voice to the intangible:

I can say, perhaps, that it's tormented me
or it may be wrong to say that it's tormented me
it's more as if
Oh I don't know
It's more as if it's been there
all my life
like a question
like a call
For we found the way to each other
and then
just as suddenly and unexpectedly as we found each other
we had to part
from each other
But that's life
It's something you have to live with
It's the way
life is

The question Fosse asks me – and I can think of no other playwright who does so as radically – is whether it is possible to live with such uncertainty. In *Nightsongs*, the answer is a categorical no: here the man has no future and takes his life. But in *A Summer's Day* time is not static: instead it breaks up the space, bursting its physical boundaries. Even the rhythm of the sentences turns its back on death, like waves pounding the shore, making the words echo their pulse:

> And I stood there
> feeling how I became more and more empty
> I became empty
> like the rain and the darkness
> like the wind and the trees
> like the sea out there
> Now I was no longer uneasy
> Now I was just a great empty calm
> Now I was the darkness
> a black darkness
> Now I was nothing
> And at the same time I felt that
> well in a way there was light inside me
> Deep inside
> from the empty darkness
> I felt the light of that empty darkness
> very still
> meaning nothing
> saying nothing
> the darkness shone from inside me
> And I stood there
> by the window
> and my friend stood next to me
> and she didn't know what to say
> she just stood there
> it was all she could do
> and time passed
> but I don't think I noticed
> I stood there looking at the darkness and the rain
> and then
> my friend walked over and sat down

But I remained standing
And I looked towards
the wind and the rain and the darkness
and I felt that the darkness was my face
I don't know how long I stood there
But I stood looking out into the empty darkness
towards the rain out there
and I felt I couldn't part from the darkness
and then
I opened the window
and I could hear the rain and the wind
so much better
and I could hear the waves
hear the waves pound
the waves pounded and pounded
and I stood there
hearing the waves pound and pound
and I could feel the waves
pound through the rain and the darkness
that was now me
that would now be me
would for ever be me
Now I would be in the luminous darkness
in the pounding waves
I stood there noticing
and then I heard my girlfriend say
that I mustn't get cold standing there
I should come and sit down
I should close the window
it got so cold
she said

Depression has two faces, rather like the waves pounding above. One that condemns us to passivity and silence, sometimes death by our own hand; and another that releases us from the burden of having to assert our own self. On the one hand the despair prevalent in *Nightsongs*; on the other the ecstasy of resignation that may manifest itself when you refrain from acting, playing a part, choosing an identity, briefly: give up the idea of *being somebody*. Typical of the depressive society is the nebulous feeling of unease: you're not just unhappy, above all you're not happy, and behind this discontent is a vague sensation of living in a society made up of winners and losers. It's more about exclusion than lack of social belonging. At times these two states coincide, which makes it only more confusing. Alain Ehrenberg talks about the drug addict as a symbol of the anti-subject of our time, in days gone represented by the village fool. In *The Guitar Man*, Fosse's monologue of 1997, I find a portrait of such a contemporary prototype, a penniless busker who chooses not to mobilise his self competing with others but relies on the benevolence of passers-by.

> While I stand there in my underpass
> playing my guitar
> they pass me by
> And down at my feet
> is my open guitar case
> And some of them drop a few coins
> into my guitar case
> But most of them don't

Perhaps he's even hoping for grace considering what he says about God's angels and travelling "to an unknown town". Stripped of name and identity he stands there day after day on the street corner, singing the same old songs, a cliché transformed into the anti-hero of the post-industrial society:

I have nothing to lose
I have nothing to gain
I have nothing left
of that which gave me a future

The loss of ego is the sombre outcome of the depressive society, the reverse of the identity hunt exhorting us to realise ourselves at any cost. The motto of the 1990s was in fact *identity*. In the Balkans we saw it lead to war when different ethnic groups searched for their roots in religion, language, nation or culture, that is, in the past. Our own identity hunt is more about the future and our own self. Choose your identity, we are told: create it, give yourself a brand, a logo.

Fosse's plays can be read and performed as a criticism of the society where these ideals gain ground. But it has to be emphasized that this criticism is indirect, he is not a traditional social critic, not a polemicist, only an opponent of the stale language of officialdom. Social ills are not his department. But we see them as shadows, as black holes in the landscape. His characters keep saying about each other that they disappear, slip away, die; as in these quotes taken at random from different plays:

Don't go
- - -
She's disappearing in front of my eyes
- - -
Let's go
- - -
We're not staying
- - -
You mustn't disappear like that
- - -
And you just go away
- - -
We can't stay here

\- - -

Where are you going

\- - -

I have nowhere to go

\- - -

He left

\- - -

I'm leaving

\- - -

Come back soon

\- - -

I just want to go away

The meaning is both literal – the characters really move on and off the stage – and an expression of time's enigmatic presence in our lives. The loss is felt long before it has actually happened.

> But he
> he's walking straight into his own death
> Did you not see him
> Don't you see what's happening
> He's dying
> He's dying here
> right in front of our eyes
> He walks away from everything
> from his own life
> from everything
> He's walking straight into his own death
> He won't make it
> He disappears
> He

This phenomenon – death in the middle of life – is something we can never escape from, and just as it fills us with terror, it opens up a possibility of *resisting* the social demands imposed upon us by anonymous people in authority. The modern society is not absent in these plays, but its presence is only indirect, in contrast to the events we see taking place on stage.

Fosse's myth is not that of Oedipus but of Antigone, the king's daughter prevented by Creon to bury her dead brother. Antigone is always seen as a symbol of conscience and righteousness: she rebels against the laws of the state and refuses to compromise. But that is a simplistic view of Sophocles' play. In Antigone's stubborn resistance to every thought of compromise there is a strange darkness. After all she welcomes death and goes to the grave as to her own bridal chamber to collect, as she says, her "reward".

> Grave, which will be my bridal chamber, you eternal
> dwelling sunk deep into the earth, where I go
> to meet my loved ones

Antigone's civil courage is but one side of her war against Creon and the interests of the state. The other is her longing for death, and if there is an Antigone complex in Fosse's dramatic work, it relates to the freedom and intimacy experienced by king Oedipus' daughter when she is close to death. This doesn't necessarily blunt the tragedy. But it indicates a path away from it – and an alternative: mysticism.

9. THE WIND BLOWS WHERE IT WILL

My first thought after seeing *The Child* at the National Theatre in Oslo in 1996 was that Jon Fosse must be a Catholic. Something about the darkness and the sudden transition to a merciful light associated strongly to the Catholic belief in miracles. I asked a Norwegian literary scholar, who I thought ought to know, about Fosse's attitude to Catholicism: he dismissed my speculations with a line that I was astonished to hear in a Fosse play only a couple of years later:

> But that's what they are like
> these people from the West Country

It didn't make sense to me, for what I thought I had discovered in *The Child* differed from the strict coastal piety found in places like Norway's West Country and the Hebrides, where the closeness to the elements often fostered a strict submission to God. My associations were more to a wordless dimension of miracles and grace than to the ascetic ideals of Puritanism. Could I have been so mistaken?

The remote bus stop in the first scene is next to a church with a cross on its brick wall. A man, said to be about fifty and called Arvid, appears briefly. A collector of empty bottles, rather like God collecting souls, he is one of those Beckett-type figures and odd existences that Fosse liberally incorporates into his world. Agnes and Fredrik, the young couple who meet here by chance, decide to enter the church. Although neither of them believes in God – even though they occasionally say a prayer – they are attracted to this sanctuary: to seal, in Agnes' words, "that they have found each other".

It's our wedding day
We met today
And we're getting married today
Entirely in our own way
Come along

Later on they do get married and move into a flat; she
becomes pregnant and gives birth to a daughter, whose life can't
be saved. In the final scene we are back at the bus stop. Arvid is
sitting there in his padded jacket with the shoulder bag between
his feet. Agnes and Fredrik come out of the church after the
child's funeral and soon walk on, while, according to the stage
direction, it becomes *gradually lighter and lighter*, not – as more
usual in contexts such as these – *gradually darker, lights down,
black out.*

No one can ignore the theme of resurrection in Fredrik's
speech about the dead child as someone they will always
remember and keep alive:

I shall always remember her
Her hands
Her face
Her hands looking like mine
Her face looking like yours
In any case I shall remember
I shall remember till the day I die
even long after I die
I shall remember
She will be alive in me
I shall let her live

He says so with a simple conviction that I find difficult to
relate to the Lutheran form of Christianity. Just as I felt Jon
Fosse was far from Ingmar Bergman's dualistic, conflict-filled
Christianity stamped by Luther's idea of God, I felt he was
close to the Catholic-inspired view of life that I had detected

with several European film directors, such as Robert Bresson, Roberto Rossellini and Pier Paolo Pasolini.

The remarkable thing about this Norwegian author, the greatest after Ibsen, is the fact that, apart from Beckett, I have found few modern playwrights comparable and related to him. His sincerity defies the extroversion of theatre, and also the theatrical urge to explain, its *horror vacui*. That is probably why many people feel confused when confronted with him.

Film is different. The thief in *Pickpocket*, Bresson's masterpiece, is saved by love after being convicted and accepting his guilt. The prisoner of war in *A Man Escaped* achieves freedom while the Kyrie in Mozart's *Requiem* heralds his second birth. In the same way, the main character in *Ladies of the Bois de Boulogne* finds grace after a life as a high-class prostitute. There are obvious similarities between the low-key dramaturgy of Bresson's films and the unexpected change of scene that makes the tragedy in *The Child* a paradoxically comforting event. It's not faith in God that saves people but God finding them: living hidden in reality when it happens, they are saved by a grace they did not ask for.

The motto of Bresson's *A Man Escaped* is a Bible quotation from John 3:8, where Jesus talks to Nicodemus the pharisee: "The wind blows where it will". This could just as well have been the title of *The Child* – but hardly of *Nightsongs* with its suicide and terrible end. The question is how to interpret this peripeteia: Is *Nightsongs* a pessimistic paraphrase of the earlier play?

I think this is the wrong question to ask. Fosse has never written dramas of ideas, he does not represent either political or religious opinions. All his work is a balance between darkness and light, between nihilism and resurrection. Even in his next play, *A Summer's Day*, this contradiction – if it can be called a contradiction – has been reduced to give way to a more even distribution of darkness, light and shadow, so even that the secret of Fosse's dramaturgy appears to be enclosed in the very undulation of his dialogue.

The lonely woman waits for the man who, several years ago, went out in his boat and never came back. Just like the sea out there, the play moves back and forth between two levels of time. The two main characters, the woman and her friend, are both split into two characters, one young and one old. When one acts, the other melts into the background or exits, as if then and now could be folded into each other, aided by retrospection and parallel scenes. The older woman witnesses what the younger one did when Asle, the man, opened the door, went down to the shore, got into his boat and disappeared:

> And I stood there
> *Looks towards the younger woman*
> looking out after him
> saw him walk down the road
> to the sea
> but he didn't turn round
> and suddenly I felt uneasy
> overcome by a peculiar unease

Asle appears on stage only in the retrospective scenes, but the memory of his disappearance imbues the play with sadness. We see a second transformed into eternity. In Fosse's writing it becomes more and more clear that form and theme condition each other. The living and the dead pass invisible borders, appear side by side, as children and parents address each other across time and space.

Nearly all his plays after *A Summer's Day* seem to have one single aim: to peel off layers in order to accommodate something else, not with a view to eliminate but to approach the point where transformation can occur, from darkness to light. And this is where another trait of Fosse's equipment emerges: mysticism. It had always been there, but only as a suggestion.

Nihilism is not absent in this process: on the contrary, it's one of its preconditions. The woman at the window in *A Summer's Day* has seen her husband disappear, probably to take his life. His long, lonesome trips in the boat are a matter of, in his own words, seeking the "danger" he experiences as "safety": a paradox shedding light over his suicide. She wants to know why he spends so many hours at sea:

> But are you not happy here
> Is there something wrong with me
> Don't you like to be
> with me
> What is it
> What's the matter with you
> You're always so restless
> never at peace
> Always want to go out on the sea

He has no reply, and perhaps this loss for words is the answer, the insight that words are inadequate. He replies with a number of self-abnegating statements taking away the meaning and explanatory power of speech:

> It's not that
> But it's so silent here
> It's so quiet
> it makes me uneasy
> to be here
> I might say
> *He laughs a little*
> Oh I don't know

With this repeated "I don't know", Fosse approaches the ecstasy of liberation that emerges when we don't have to find answers to the inquisitorial *why*. Silence, said to be his distinctive mark, is not so much about being unable to communicate as being unwilling: perhaps you have to be silent to be truthful! Behind the careful language typical of so many of Fosse's characters, another of these reluctant 'not' can be surmised: a rejection of expression in the restrictive terms of language and, above all, speech.

In other words, seeing him as 'a playwright of the lack of communication' is gravely simplistic, a cliché fed by the therapeutic society and its blind faith in confession and uninterrupted conversation as an open sesame to the inner world of a human being. What if it's really the other way round – that speech serves to conceal rather than reveal? Telling lies instead of the truth?

One of Fosse's essays gives guidance to those who search for an understanding of the silences in his plays: "So the best thing with which to surround your deepest knowledge may be silence. It may be also silent in itself, like the untold in the told. And in that case it may be enlightening that your deepest knowledge is not something you can produce and argue in favour of, it is too silent for that, in the way that it is simply something you know. How you come to know it and why and all that is less interesting. It is probably wiser just to let it be, indeterminate, in your writing."

Fosse's silence is not in a psychological category, and for that reason has nothing to say about the reasons why his characters are silent or give evasive answers. It doesn't mean that the psychological landscape is lacking in his rendering of totally trivial situations: inhibitions, insecurity, feelings of being unreal, alienation between children and parents; however, one feels like saying, in his own words: *all that is less interesting.*

In the writings of Meister Eckhart, the greatest and most influential of medieval Christian mystics, two concepts appear that may illuminate Fosse's negations. One is the concept of *abgeschiedenheit*, in medieval German *abegescheidenheit*, which can be translated as 'separateness', even if its reach goes considerably further. It does not mean asceticism but more a fundamental freedom, not viewing life passively but preparing actively to merge with God.

The other concept, another of Eckhart's linguistic innovations, is *sunder warumbe*, which means 'without why'. In the same way as *abgeschiedenheit*, the act of separating, aims at making man rest within himself, we must allow God to rest within himself. God, who is not distinguished by any aim, is identified by this 'let it be' (*gelazenheit*), which cannot be explained and does not respond to any 'why'.

Quite simply, being *is*. Only by emptying yourself and not producing answers, can man get to know God.

Such an emptying of the self is found in most forms of Christian mysticism. Meister Eckhart bases one of his Latin sermons on Saul's vision of God in The Acts of the Apostles 9:8: "And Saul arose from the earth, and when his eyes were opened, he saw no man." Eckhart's God is nothing other than this Nothing. In explosive paradoxes he defines and captures the essence of God: "The light that is God shines in the darkness. God is the real light; to see it you have to be blind and keep God at a distance from whatever it is".

When about a fifth of *A Summer's Day* remains and the fluctuation between then and now resumes, it becomes obvious that Fosse is well versed in this *via negativa* of mysticism. The older woman turns away from the window and releases her thoughts in one long monologue, where she describes how one time she stood in the same place looking out for the man who had disappeared at sea. This is Jon Fosse's version of Meister Eckhart's *sunder warumbe*:

> Now I was no longer uneasy
> Now I was just a great empty calm
> Now I was the darkness
> a black darkness
> Now I was nothing
> And at the same time I felt that

well in a way there was light inside me
Deep inside
from the empty darkness
I felt the light of that empty darkness
very still
meaning nothing
saying nothing
the darkness shone from inside me

In its most radical form, the *via negativa* of mysticism has the essence of God not as an object to view, nothing we direct our eyes *towards*, not something we can believe *in*. All the prepositions melt away on the threshold between Nothing and this light, which merely exists, as sudden as in the lines of this monologue: Now I was nothing/And at the same time I felt that/ well in a way there was light inside me.

Christian mysticism diverges into two branches: the *cataphatic*, or positive, which makes positive statements about God as the highest truth and goodness, and the *apophatic*, negative, which sees speech as a hindrance to knowledge of God's being. Sooner or later, the *via negativa* reaches the point where Eckhart's paradoxes become valid, for if God is unknowable, inaccessible to language, he can only be captured in incomplete sentences; or hardly even then, since the known language cannot do more than confirm its powerlessness: "He is the nothing of nothing, he is neither this nor that".

The inadequacy of language also stops the tradition of mysticism from appearing in a pure form. It has many tributaries. In Christian mysticism prior to Eckhart, the doctrine of Jesus is joined by Gnosticism, Platonism and neo-Platonism. Even in early Jewish mysticism there is a symbolism of darkness and light reminiscent of the Christian kind. Both the sixth-century mystic Dionysus the Areopagite and the authors of the anonymous medieval work *The Cloud of Unknowing* talk of the path to God through the darkness of silence and 'not-knowing'.

In the writings of twentieth-century mystics such as Thomas Merton and Pierre Teilhard de Chardin, it is obvious that the *via negativa* is close to the Buddhist concept of emptiness.

Meister Eckhart does not have a monopoly on the *gelazenheit* he preaches. But his wordings have an amazing suggestive power. He rebels against the limited reach of words and testifies to it as the poet facing Nothing. Eckhart was not only a theologian and a philosopher: he was a master of language who, faced with a precipice of meaninglessness, retrieved a remainder of meaning from verbal destitution. The Swedish poet, literary scholar and Academy member Anders Olsson writes pointedly of Eckhart's *via negativa*: "Overwhelmed by the experience of God, the mystic is prompted to remarkable utterances that often, though not always, are aware of their own impossibility. The word is ejected, only to be instantly recalled".

The rediscovery of Meister Eckhart by the Romanticists brought the heritage further into the modern era. From Hegel and Heidegger, who took an interest in the concept of *Gelassenheit* ('Letting be'), the *via negativa* of mysticism can be traced to Jon Fosse, who writes in one of his essays that his own experiences of mysticism "are connected with writing", to what you leave to the reader; it was through the "grace" of literature that he himself became aware of "abandoning himself to the hands of both the others and the other".

Cadences appear in *The Guitar Man*, where the trustful busker finds evangelical expression for a sign language that is both contemporary and universal:

> Let me become
> a nothing
> and let that song sound
> Let me become
> an unknown sign
> for others to interpret

Fosse is a mystic. But in his case, too, influence comes from different directions. He is not a theologian disguised as a poet. The close connection between nihilism and mysticism is such an exceedingly modern literary experience that he can formulate his own contribution amidst a stream of generally held views and more extreme doctrines. If Fosse is to be placed in a wider context, it will have to be in the main furrow of Romanticism and its extension into twentieth-century Modernism, embracing Kierkegaard, Baudelaire, Schopenhauer, Rilke and Mallarmé, and also Nordic poets and prose writers such as Edith Södergran, Gunnar Ekelöf, Mirjam Tuominen, Karl Vennberg and Birgitta Trotzig.

To the tradition of Fosse's mysticism has to be added the West Country Puritanism, the non-ceremonial worship of the Quakers and his childhood vacillations between imposed prohibitions and rebellion against authority. He himself has admitted the influence of Puritanism on his thinking and writing ("I suppose I'm a kind of post-Puritan, actually in the company of Samuel Beckett, the author most influenced by the Quakers.")

In *Mother and Child* we saw the son's fragile self-esteem anchored in an idealised image of his grandmother and her deep faith "in herself and her Lord Jesus Christ". Perhaps Fredrik's and Agnes' salvation in *The Child* is an example of a similar suddenly recovered childhood faith when they meet for the first time in the obscurity of the bus shelter and enter the empty church. "And then you came to believe in God", as the nurse says to Fredrik, amazed that it was luck, not bad luck, that brought them in this direction:

> Usually it's the other way round
> That when something goes wrong
> people
> kind of
> turn to God

Fredrik's reply reveals to him and – supposedly – to the author the inexplicable nature of this event:

> It sounds so
> ridiculous
> But
> *Stops himself*
> But I suppose that's it

The experience of God needs no reason:

> I experienced something
> and then something kind of happened to me

Of Meister Eckhart's linguistic innovations, it is above all *sunder warumbe* that leads us straight into Fosse's world. What we see in *A Summer's Day* is not a symbolically described apparition of the kind seen in *The Child*, where the church with its cross can hardly be misunderstood. It is more like the *without why* of mysticism, at once frightening and secure. Asle's suicide remains inconceivable. He cannot answer his wife's questions. It's beyond language. In the end she, too, is reconciled with his "I don't know" when the darkness becomes luminous "meaning nothing" and "saying nothing", that is, without answering her why, as if time itself offered this grace to her as well.

Everywhere in Fosse's plays we are given the same evasive answers. For example, the daughter in *Visits* – she goes around on her own, has no friends, locks herself into her room – has no answer to her mother's question why she doesn't do her schoolwork. "I don't know". She may be a typical teenager of the kind we've seen in recent years in Lukas Moodysson's *Show Me Love* and numerous other films and television series. Fosse has a good eye for the vulnerability of young people – children constantly reappear in his portrayals of existential borderline conditions. The step into the adult world is the most difficult in a person's life. But the lack of connection he explores is different from the usual form: it can't be adjusted, it's not a theme for psychologists, therapists and crisis handlers. Siv, as the girl is called, is born to this world; it's hardly worthwhile asking why. In short, she *is*, lives and exists, and when finally she leaves home, her brother asks her if it isn't sad that so little will remain of their life together:

> It's a bit sad
> don't you think
> that your room
> our room
> is quite empty
> isn't it

"Let's go then", he goes on. There's little more to add. She just smiles. From other Fosse plays we know that she will move on, from one place to another, from one room to another, to houses with peeling paint, where others have lived before and time alone will be her home.

Time is his major theme, and if he had written no other play than *Dream of Autumn*, he would still have been one of our most important contemporary dramatists. Here the setting is a graveyard and the characters a man and a woman, his mother and father and his wife Gry. As the play opens they are married. After a number of script pages it emerges that they are divorced. Soon the parents arrive to bury the man's grandmother. A little later we understand that his father, too, has died, just like his son and finally, the man himself. The three women remain: the mother, Gry and the new woman, whom he meets at the beginning of the play.

What we witness is a long chain of events compressed to the physical duration of the play on stage (normally between sixty and ninety minutes). As we watch, the characters live, die and take part in constellations extending over several years.

Isn't that what happens in all theatre? That time and space are the medium of the scenic event? Of course, but Fosse writes *about time itself*. Without any introduction or finished scenes, *Dream of Autumn* becomes a play where the present is dissolving at every moment. Fosse's idea is to conceive and portray the disappearance of life. What's dying all the time is the present. When the three women finally get up and walk off, arm in arm, along one of the gravel paths of the graveyard, one of them gets to say:

> Well
> *Pause*
> He got up
> and then he was dead
> *Pause*
> I can't believe that he is dead
> that he is gone
> for ever

Death is here both physical – the grandmother is being buried, the father really dies – and existential, that is, death as a fundamental condition of life, the loss carried by each and every second, distancing us from ourselves and from others. "You mustn't go" they urge one another. "You mustn't disappear". Nobody seems to appear at the right moment, all the time they are waiting for someone who ought to turn up, if two are together a third is missing. "Well it's about time now", says the father in one of his few lines, as if the flow of time could be stopped and divided into finished moments. Expressions such as 'long ago', 'return' and 'early on' wrap themselves around each other to form the dialogue's own melancholy chord:

> And I tell you
> that often
> when I want to die
> I think of you

And then, now and again I feel you're there
Now and again I feel
nothing
and then you're not there
but you're often there
and I want to die when I feel you there
more often than when I don't feel you there

Unlike *A Dreamplay* by Strindberg, it is time, not space, that is suspended. What happens is roughly as follows: a man and a woman meet in a graveyard, they seem to know each other from before, possibly they've had an affair, and before long they talk about going to a hotel; actually, they say, they'd had a feeling that they would meet this day, as if it were predetermined. At the same time he is reluctant, because he does not want to be unfaithful to his wife, Gry, and he feels responsible towards his son, Gaute.

Soon Fosse's dream play proceeds on to the next point on this axis of time: the grandmother's funeral – as always allowing for the fact that his dramas rely on no fixed points: an entrance or exit is enough to indicate the passage of an unknown number of days, months and years. His early plays were filled with the demons of jealousy. They all escaped to new places, only to find that they weren't free. The more he writes for the stage, the clearer becomes the theme of his attention to the phenomenology of time. When the man and woman in *Dream of Autumn* go around reading on tombstones they are reminded of life's brevity, but also of the ordinariness of these lives, of the men and women who once loved and procreated, perhaps it happened, even, in this graveyard. "Perhaps it was a man who had her mother in a graveyard", the man says, pointing to a tombstone. "Perhaps she was conceived in this graveyard". As in Beckett, the woman gives birth astride a grave.

Can you hear her
groaning and screaming
Take me
Take me hard
Take me
she screamed

His fantasies make the woman toy with the idea of him doing the same to her, but he doesn't want to be unfaithful, and in the middle of this dialogue about sex and love, sneaks in the suspicion that nothing is certain, that everything passes and can be traded for its opposite. Each line in *Dream of Autumn* is reminiscent of the temporality, even triviality, of our conditions:

Won't you sit down
for a while
Do you have time
Quickly
Or perhaps you don't have the time
Perhaps you have things to do
Perhaps you're in a hurry

From here comes this fundamental distrust of language and all therapeutic aspirations that, with the help of confession and speech, we can reach the truth about ourselves and each other. The worst thing I know, says the woman, is when people "want to be so free and clever and talk about everything", and the man agrees, comparing the eager chatter about sex with that about God:

I mean it
or mean and mean
but the more you talk about it
about sex
that is
and the more you talk about

well God
the more you lose what you talk about
and in the end
only the talk remains

Note the reservation "or mean and mean". Related as it is to
sunder warumbe, it expresses above all a message that what is
and what we take for granted will never last. Time opens up a
gap in the language. "You mustn't disappear", the woman calls
to the man, and in this 'disappear' is something else, more than
fear of him abandoning her the way he abandoned Gry:

I get so scared
There's something
What is it
In despair
You mustn't disappear

Fosse's version of jealousy is nothing other than the law of
the inescapable disappearance of everything. You don't possess
your loved one because you don't possess time. But just as with
Meister Eckhardt, it does not lead to resignation or resentment,
but rather to flaring paradoxes, verbal exchanges defying logic.
The dialogue in *Dream of Autumn* is pervaded by mystical
reversals and replacements:

Nothing is the same thing
- - -
And it's all the same thing
- - -
It's all a game
- - -
And it's all serious
- - -
It's all a serious game
- - -

We have to go home

- - -

We have no home

- - -

You must take me

- - -

I don't know if I want to take you

- - -

All is long ago

- - -

Nothing is long ago

Everything happens at the same time as it evaporates. In this process yet another dimension of Fosse's theatre opens up, related to mysticism but with a history of its own: Gnosticism, the doctrine regarding earth as a home for strangers, a place you long to leave.

10. NEAR AND YET SO FAR

*D*ream *of Autumn* opens with a man and a woman meeting by chance in a graveyard. They are at once surprised and not surprised, partly because they know each other – which is clear from the first line: "Oh it's you" – partly because the reader or the spectator immediately starts to doubt whether this is true. What is chance seems to harbour a secret intention, the unexpected slowly turning into its opposite: "Actually, I thought of you before coming here".

This type of mystery occurs time and again in Fosse's plays; the feeling that everything that happens is both natural and supernatural. When we ourselves have such an experience, a warning bell usually sounds. We know it's superstition. August Strindberg had no such scruples: the older he became, the keener he was to identify signs of the deceptive quality of chance:

"When finally I am without food and plan to jump into the river, I find something to eat in the street. It can't be chance, so what is it? – It's something else, but how it happens we can't possibly know, as we know so little about the most trivial things. – Ah, nonsense. 'Crex Crex' – Is that the corncrake? – Yes it is."

The notion that something other than chance controls our destiny helped Strindberg see life as a drama. We all partake in a plot shaped by a storyteller, a weaver with the thread of destiny in his hand or – when he is in that mood – by an evil producer, the Demiurge. In *The Great Highway* events like these occur all the time.

Strindberg blamed 'the powers that be'. Fosse would hardly do that, but a hint of Strindberg's chamber plays can be detected in *Dream of Autumn*, where a man and a woman are brought together in what looks like a scenario. Although, as she says, they "never had much to do with each other", they've gone around in life longing to meet. Their appearance at the same time in this spot seems inexplicable, as if a strange hand watched over their lives:

> To think
> well I thought
> that perhaps I'd run into you
> when I went out
> It's true
> I thought so
> quite clearly
> I knew I'd run into you
> Isn't that strange
> *The man nods*
> Very strange

The graveyard in *Dream of Autumn* has, come to think of it, the same metaphorical function as the burnt-out property in Strindberg's chamber play *The Burned House*, where The Stranger picks through the ashes with his stick and sees a life pattern take shape. Asked where he got this idea, The Stranger elaborates in terms that could be taken from one of Fosse's plays:

> Because, however life turned out – I have been rich and poor, high and low, suffered shipwreck and earthquake; however life turned out, I always found a pattern and a recurrence – in one situation I saw the result of another preceding it; meeting one person I was reminded of someone else in my past. There are even scenes in my life that have recurred several times, so that I've often told myself: I've been through this before. And some events have appeared to me quite inescapable or predestined.

There is little point in suggesting a direct influence by the late Strindberg on Fosse – it's more a matter of a tradition that started with, amongst others, Strindberg and then became part of the formal language of modern drama. A more immediate connection is in the interest shown by both these authors in Christian and other mysticism, in the case of Strindberg, Buddhism and Indian philosophy. Fosse certainly distances himself from the type of eschatology present in Strindberg's chamber plays, where concepts such as suffering, guilt, punishment and reconciliation are central themes. Nevertheless, the many points in common can be summed up in a more general concept of life awareness, as in the Strindberg quotation above: "There are even scenes in my life that have recurred several times, so that I've often told myself: I've been through this before."

In Strindberg's writing, the feeling of self is challenged by the encounter with nature, with other people and with the powers that be. In Fosse's plays, the ego is too weak to bend. Since it does not rebel, neither does it need to go through the process of punishment and salvation that is the way to Christian conversion in Strindberg's conspiratorial view of the world: I suffer, thus I'm guilty.

Neither is Ibsen's life battle on the cards when Fosse's characters are faced with deathly cold in their hearts. They may leave their home, but they don't slam the door behind them like Nora in *A Doll's House*. The joy of life and happiness that Ibsen's characters refer to has its roots in Romanticism and the nineteenth-century discovery of the inner person, as Michael Goldman writes in his thin but significant volume *Ibsen, The Dramaturgy of Fear*. More than anything they abhor emptiness and seek to establish a connection with the help of passion. To come alive inside – "in the arcs of heart and brain", according to Ibsen – is the moral and sensual duty facing us, not unlike Rilke's poetic exhortation: "Du muß dein Leben ändern" (You must change your life).

In Fosse's plays, a feeling of emptiness prevails. His characters are not vitalised when they find themselves in a crisis. They don't call out like Rosmer in Ibsen's drama: "Give me back my faith!" – or with Rebecka: "Take up the fight once more, Johannes!" And with emptiness follow anonymity and homelessness. The man in *Dream of Autumn* says that he lives near the graveyard, but the woman has only just arrived by air, as if a cosmic planetary journey were needed for this chance meeting to take place. Even the graveyard gives an impression of being suspended high above the surrounding city. When she points to the houses and talks about all those who are there, who live, die and are replaced, we see everything through the eye of God.

> By and by all people are replaced
> by other people
> they are all replaced
> I say to myself
> and if you look back
> a hundred years back
> well not even that far
> completely different people
> were in the city
> walked the streets
> but the city is there
> the houses are there

The factors determining the man's life – his divorce, the death of his son – are mentioned only in passing. His identity is unknown just like hers, neither place nor year are relevant, only the age and ageing of the characters indicate the passing of time. At the same time as Fosse deals with the most trivial things, the feeling of presence is suspended. They are here – but do they belong here?

> But he
> he's walking straight into his own death
> Did you not see him
> Don't you see what's happening
> He's dying
> He's dying here

right in front of our eyes
He walks away from everything
from his own life
from everything
He's walking straight into his own death
He won't make it
He disappears
He

What kind of death is this? He simply leaves the stage and disappears, as it is said. It's hardly the physical death that Fosse addresses in *Dream of Autumn* and related pieces like *Death Variations*, *Sleep* and *Shadows*, where the characters constantly 'leave' in the double meaning of withdrawing and dying. When the words 'die' and 'disappear' in the quote from the play above are added to each other, the factual meaning becomes metaphorical, and this is how Fosse writes all the time – to enable us to see, as in double exposure, how time and space are not static, how everything is moving, dissolving, disappearing, 'dying'.

Fosse's theatre relies on this conception of time. It becomes clearer the further his writing progresses: what started out as a theme gradually becomes a principle of form, a fundamental pattern in his dramaturgy. I believe you have to go to Augustine's famous reflection on the essence of time in the eleventh book of his *Confessions* to find the origin of Fosse's thoughts:

"So what is time? If no one asks me that, I know; if someone asks me and I want to explain it to him, then I don't know – but I'm still convinced that I know that there would be no past if nothing had happened, no future if nothing followed, no present if nothing was going on. So how can these two times – the past and the future – exist, when the past is no more and the future is not yet? But if the present were always present and did not pass into the past, then it would no longer be the present but eternity. If the on-going becomes time only by passing into the past, how can we say that even the present exists, when the premise for its existence is that it will be no more? Are we not really saying that time exists just because it strives not to be?"

In *Dream of Autumn*, human existence is but a parenthesis in a larger, less tangible, extended context. The present as a finite phenomenon does not exist, it is dying all the time. Mysticism offers a promise of liberation from death in the heart of life. The words, while signifying nothingness and emptiness, also suggest something else:

> Beyond there is nothing
> and then the light

However, this mysticism does not operate on its own. Another, equally important element in Fosse's search for a dramaturgy representing the presence of time in human existence comes from the ideology of Gnosticism. The homelessness that prevails in each line of these texts is the Gnostic idea of life on earth as a hiding-place for darkness, sleep and alienation, in contrast to the eternal light of the true essence of God.

The influence of Gnosticism on Western ideology is not easy to pinpoint precisely, but it cannot be overestimated. We are often reached by Gnostic ideas in an eclectic mix, which reflects its early history. The philosopher Hans Jonas, author of a classic work on Gnosticism, perceives Hellenistic, Christian, Coptic, non-Orthodox Jewish and Oriental elements blended into a doctrine rejected by the Church but maintaining its attraction for generations of heretics and, in our time, intellectuals (Jonas mentions, amongst others, Heidegger).

Decisive for the Gnostic perception of the world is a dualistic view of the world of nature, animals and human beings as created, not by God but by a lower power (the Demiurge). According to this ideology, God is completely alien, accessible only through special knowledge, *gnosis*, not scientific knowledge of a factual concept, the Greek *logos*, but a more privileged kind of knowledge, accessible only to a few initiates; *gnosis* is more akin to the mystical view of the essence of God, though more exclusive, less attainable. This explains the dualism. God's world is entirely one of light and has no connection with our existence, which is ruled by darkness, just like sleep, paralysis, extinction.

It is enough to point out two themes of Gnostic origin in most of Fosse's work for the stage. One is sleep and fatigue, the burden many of his characters seem to be carrying. The other is alienation, the feeling of belonging nowhere. As early as *Someone Will Arrive*, the man and woman lie down on the bed, close together, terrified by the fantasies brought to mind by their isolation.

This choreography of prostration is repeated in *And We Shall Never Part*, where the man comes home and says that he is "quite tired", while the woman lies down, her head on his lap, promising that they can soon go to bed; though there is no mention of sex, just rest:

> Wouldn't that be nice
> To lie in bed
> You and I
> next to each other
> Lie there next to each other
> next to each other in bed

There is a strange prevalence of the 'horizontal' in Fosse's plays, of rest and night, sleep and numbness. In *The Name* there is much talk of lying down: "It was nice seeing you but I think I must go and lie down again". The father, mother, Beate, the boyfriend and the sister: all have a need to withdraw and rest: "No I'm too tired". At a certain level, the social field of vision coincides with the existential in these realistic portrayals of a working-class environment with room for little other than the struggle to make a living. Fosse never writes about the urban middle-class chasing the kicks and survival tips of lifestyle magazines. His characters survive as best they can.

At the same time, there is another aspect to this passivity: the torpor of sleep has no connection to problems in society. The failed author in *Nightsongs* spends his days lying on the sofa before committing suicide. Even if his depressive state could be contained within the framework of therapeutic diagnoses, he suffers from an affliction that cannot be diagnosed: he is one of these sleepwalkers waiting to be awakened.

The material existence in Gnostic iconography is immersed in coma, lethargy, listlessness. An original unity has been reduced to fragments. We who walk here in darkness are not-knowing beings who, in the best of cases, can be enlightened. From God to the lowest levels of the cosmos, a range of intermediaries, so called aeons, extends. A spark of the true light can be concealed within each one of us, feeding a vague feeling that we are lacking something, that we are half-beings, neither alive nor dead.

Most Gnostic myths and systems imagine a stranger, an Alien, descending to the human world to examine whether we are prepared to rise and return. But first we have to be awakened, since we are asleep! It explains the longing and the attraction existing between the Alien and the familiar, between him and the blinded crowds walking in darkness here. For most beings, this Alien is invisible, only to a few chosen ones does he appear familiar, a God's emissary looking for someone he can bring back with him:

Nice to see you

The person speaking this line in *Death Variations* is called The Friend and is, from, beginning to end, a Gnostic invention, an anonymous being – he could just as well have been called The Stranger – moving on the margin of the other characters. The Daughter answers him in the same colloquial manner:

Yeah
Happily
yeah that was great

In spite of this familiar type of chat they don't know each other, though that, too, seems uncertain: "Perhaps," says The Friend, "we have known each other a long time". Compare the inception of *Dream of Autumn*, where the man and woman get together in a similar vague meeting. In *Death Variations*, the happening is even more unreal. The Daughter and The Friend say that they both know and do not know each other – to her "I'm not sure" he replies with the typical Fosse word 'perhaps':

Or perhaps we have just always
known each other
It may well be like that

Phrases are repeated and varied in a mixture reminiscent of inconsequential chatter. "We probably have". But in the middle of the familiarity he warns her that he has to go, as if he posed a danger to a teenage girl. When the play begins, The Daughter is already dead and mourned by her parents, who suffer from not understanding *why*. Her suicide is the enigma of the play. "That she could do it". Now and then, in Fosse's by now well-established manner, time changes place; the two parental figures are divided into The Older Woman and The Older Man and The Young Woman and The Young Man respectively.

In other words, there is no fixed *now*. Still, it would be a mistake to call the scenes with the young parents retrospective. That would assume that there was an absolute present to start from, as if The Daughter's suicide took place in the past and they were missing her in the present. This present – as Augustine teaches us – is nothing but a fiction, a present already split into the small constituents of time.

In any case, the character of The Friend is different: he is invisible to all except the girl. He is the Alien who has come to collect her. The spark lit between them lights up the darkness here on earth. "She is no longer with you", he says to the old couple. "She is with me". Without his invisibility cloak he would not be this semi-transparent stranger, with whom only the young girl can establish contact, which becomes apparent when she finally goes with him, towards the sea, continues over the edge of the quay, to be found later, dead in the water. "She followed her death", as her father says.

Her suicide is like that of Asle in *A Summer's Day*, the man who feels safe when he can be alone at sea where the water is very deep, and who does not return from his fishing trip. The suicide in *Death Variations* may not be surrounded by the same restful deliberation. In the last line of the play, The Daughter voices regrets, but here, too, in amidst the sadness, there is an ambivalence, a longing both for darkness and light.

> I want to go back
> I want to be alone again
> I shouldn't have

The event as such, the meeting with The Friend in particular, is not given a closer explanation. It is Fosse's way of portraying the longing that pervades all that lives. "I shall always be your friend," says the Young Man to the Young Woman (i.e. the girl's future parents). "I'm so glad I met you." The Daughter and The Friend are by no means exceptional. Any line spoken by them could just as well have been spoken by the others, as the six characters in the play slowly intermingle and reflect each other. Within each living being is an ambivalence, an attraction connecting opposites, between being and not being, darkness and light, sleep and wake.

Your friend! It could be any one of us.

Mysticism and Gnosticism enlighten this world and this life, not the next one. That is how I interpret the paradoxes in *Death Variations*:

We stand there always
And we stand there never
And it's somewhat good
And somewhat evil
- - -
And all is long ago
and all has just happened
And it doesn't matter
what we do
or don't
- - -
I shall never return
I shall always return
- - -
We are both far from each other
And quite close to each other
That's how it is

Gnostic ideas have always been present in Fosse's work, although they become more prevalent as of *Dream of Autumn* and *Death Variations*. The child expected by Beate in *The Name* exists somewhere else before coming to earth to be given its name. Names generally are important to Fosse, who lets the woman in *Dream of Autumn* reveal that, on her way to the graveyard, she met a girl who stated that "all pretty names are boring". It could be said that Jon Fosse's Gnosticism is of a naïve variety, a kind of brooding that I think most of us recognize, an amazed wonder at the existence of the universe and ourselves.

However, this calls for a reservation. As we have seen, the Gnostic doctrine is distinguished by uncompromising dualism. God's light comes from elsewhere altogether, with no nuances between darkness and light. And it has to be emphasized that all forms of dualism are alien to Fosse. He would be more likely to say, like the Swedish author and Quaker Emilia Fogelklou: "What lives needs no proof. It appears. It is."

So how does this relate to Gnostic ideology? I think it can be explained by the considerable influence that Gnosticism has on all Western philosophy and literature. It would be misguiding to suggest that Fosse *is* a Gnostic. But his writing has its roots in the legacy of Romanticism and its extension into the main literary furrow of Modernism, where Gnostic ideas are present, if more or less pronounced. So in his essentially non-dualist perspective, the Gnostic legacy emerges. But he writes about this world as if it were the only one that exists, with a deep tenderness for all that lives in it.

11. IN THE WORLD

Reading *Sleep* long before it's due to open, directed by Sophia Jupiter at the National Theatre in Oslo in the autumn of 2005, I try to imagine ways of enacting it. As usual, Fosse's demands on director and actors are almost superhuman. The cast includes ten characters, most of whom are the same people but at different stages in their lives. He goes further than in *A Summer's Day* and *Death Variations*, where he first tried this approach, extending time to embrace three generations. The simplest way of showing how this is envisaged is by quoting the list of characters:

> The First Young Woman
> The First Young Man
> The Second Young Woman
> The Second Young Man
> The Middle-Aged Man
> The Older Woman
> The Older Man
> The Middle-Aged Woman
> The Man
> The Son

Using the building blocks from his earlier plays, Fosse exposes them to an even more radical simplification. The set has no performing or realistic function: it's only a space where the characters appear, a stage without concrete details. We recognize the young couple in the first lines: those who enter, look around and say "This is where we shall live", two of these itinerant individuals in Fosse's world of temporary, more or less empty dwellings.

More surprising, perhaps, is the fact that another couple – The Other Young Woman and The Other Young Man – enter saying the same thing ("it took us a long time indeed to find a place to live"). Irrespective of their age, the difference between these two couples is negligible. On the whole it seems irrelevant whether they are in the same fictitious room: the script does not contain directions of any such room, and the question of the actual theme of *Sleep* could be given the brief answer: they live, grow old and die. The Older Woman falls ill, dies and is carried out on a stretcher by The Middle-Aged Man and The Older Man. The list of props is equally simplified and reduced: a pram, a wheelchair, a stretcher.

The attributes of life and death.

To understand how this non-tangible dramaturgy will find its way to the stage, I have little help from the thirty or so Fosse performances that I have seen in Norway, Sweden, Germany, Great Britain and France, not because they were unsuccessful or uninteresting – many were both bold and full of insight, some extraordinarily sensitive – but because I can't get rid of a feeling that Fosse is searching for something that still remains to be realised.

In practically all theatre, from Aeschylus and Shakespeare to Sarah Kane and Marius von Mayenburg, the actors enter and tell the audience who they portray. Even a broken psyche has a history. The pleasure of the audience is often in discovering that X is not who we thought he was or witnessing Y being made to confess who he or she really 'is'. Oedipus is a tragic example of the latter, the parricide made to discover his identity and punish himself; while Isabella in Shakespeare's *Measure for Measure* is a comic example of the former: the novice nun defending herself desperately against the idea of love and made to admit her foolish misconception.

The self-discovery is shared by actors and audience in this theatre of mirrors, where the greatest pleasure is had from recognition. We go to the theatre to learn something about ourselves and others.

What we learn from Fosse is more of an existential kind. There is something anonymous about the young, ageing and dying characters in plays like *Sleep* and *Shadows*, where the modern quest for identity is notably absent. With his radically different aesthetic, Fosse poses significant challenges to directors and actors. Many try to resolve the dilemma by normalising him: reading a history and submerged conflict into the vacuum left in the script. Each time Fosse turns his back on the psychological repertoire of clarifications and explanations, directors rush to reinstate it, as if he had forgotten to tell us that 'this has happened'. It's perfectly possible to approach David Hare, Sam Shepard or Lars Norén in this manner, since they write plays for actors trained in the system of Stanislavsky and The Actors Studio. But in an encounter with Fosse, that method is doomed to fail. A director looking for a subtext in *Sleep* and *Shadows* will find nothing but the text. The characters would only become watered-down if complemented by a life story claiming to explain the happenings on the stage. The Girl who disappears with The Friend and takes her life in *Death Variations* cannot be explained, that's the richness of the part:

> And the waves that pounded
> and pounded
> and he was so good
> he was peace
> great as love
> calm like the sea
> And heaven
> was his hand
> But I didn't want it

As far as I've been able to follow it, the story of Jon Fosse's theatre, the way he is played and understood by critics, has been an attempt to handle this dilemma. The lyrical dialogue is not the greatest hurdle, it's the choice, both aesthetic and philosophical, that becomes necessary sooner or later. His writing is so close to a fragile borderline that actors risk sabotaging it. It's comparable to the mystic's powerlessness facing the inadequacy of language, a major challenge in a profession based on the assumption that scenic expression is boosted when added to. Anyone performing Fosse has to learn to reduce and set aside their own self.

Let us return to Ostermeier's production of *The Name* at Schaubühne in Berlin. Here the interest was created mainly by the extraordinary sharpness of the portrait showing the typical, listless routines of an ordinary family, a kind of theatrical enhancement having the paradoxical effect of reducing what took place on the glum, flatly lit stage. Human life can turn out to be just as empty as this! You have been revealed! Realism seasoned with irony, also quite typical of the aesthetic mood of the 1990s. I feel Ostermeier over-interpreted the action in the play, or rather: the lack of action in it, the ordinariness pervading most days in our lives, the nameless progression from dawn to dusk: darkness, light and, again, darkness.

It's certainly true that the plays written in the period from *The Child* and *The Name* to *The Son* and *Nightsongs* are easier to read in a realistic and reasonably clear light than *Dream of Autumn*, which marks a transition in Fosse's writing. *The Son* may be the piece that comes closest to a social report. But it's a difference of degrees, not of genre. He writes for an existing theatre and is not oblivious to its traditions. *Nightsongs* could be called a modern tragedy of ruthless blackness. *The Girl on The Sofa* can be said to be as close as he ever gets to Ibsen, where an enigma of the past unfolds in successive revelations and where childhood traumas turn out to hold the key to adult shortcomings.

In 2001 and 2002 I saw two very different versions of *Dream of Autumn*, which offered much material for a discussion about ways to perform Fosse on stage: the production at Dramaten, the National Theatre in Stockholm, was by Stefan Larsson and the one at Kammerspiele in Munich by Luk Perceval. In both cases, the stage was a black box, the same as the auditorium; both plays had casts well-tuned to each other, all acting at the height of their ability, and yet the two productions were very different: heavy versus light, emotional versus moody.

In Munich, set designer Katrin Brack had a tower-like, slightly inclined cylinder placed in the middle of the stage, bringing to mind a chapel or a crematorium, but this association was rather borne out of the knowledge that the action takes place in a graveyard. Brack held back on performing detail. The pebbled floor of the stage gave the place a graphic exactitude, shifting from grey to white. The acting assumed a dry sharpness, inducing a sense of acute attentiveness, suggesting something decisive was at stake. Lines emerged, tentative and whispering, from the lips of Dagmar Manzel and Stephan Bissmeier, who played the couple meeting at the beginning of the play. The low-key style of acting would not have been possible without microphones to amplify the voices, giving the language a life of its own. Technology here achieved a reverse effect by allowing the actors to reduce their volume: we leant forward to hear, at the limits of language, where words are born, on their way out of bodily darkness.

Seeing *Dream of Autumn* in Stockholm was taking a journey to quite a different planet. First of all, Stefan Larsson had focused on the ambiance of the graveyard and the theme of death. A few crosses from graves stood out white against the dark background. No one was in any doubt that the funeral taking place in the play was a real event, while in Munich that notion had been pushed aside, more as a metaphor than a physical reality. Larsson had his interpretation tuned in a minor key. The audience was brought in through a columbarium and placed in an auditorium giving an impression of being part of the graveyard, as if we were all guests at the funeral on stage.

Secondly, the cast Larsson had chosen was obviously and securely anchored in the traditions of the National Theatre, especially in the case of the parents, played by Gunnel Lindblom and Börje Ahlstedt. They emerged from the long shadow cast by Strindberg, Ibsen and Eugene O'Neill over the style of acting on this stage, maintained and developed by Olof Molander before and after the Second World War, and followed by Ingmar Bergman, who kept it alive with his cinematically intimate interpretations.

The authority of Gunnel Lindblom's and Börje Ahlstedt's personalities could not be mistaken. Lindblom has worked with Bergman from his early films and theatre productions of the 1950s; Börje Ahlstedt was Bergman's Peer Gynt at Dramaten in 1991 and played a major role in *Fanny and Alexander*. In *Dream of Autumn* he entered as The Father, numbed by mourning, as carved out of a block of wood, clinging only to his faith in God. Although this was an amazingly skilled solo performance, the effect on the rest of the production was somewhat tautological: the word 'mourning' underlined several times.

Gunnel Lindblom played the mother just as emphatically. With a talent for the dramatic – she is easy to imagine in a Greek tragedy – she based her performance on depths of knowledge. But it was too deep, as if layers upon layers of Strindbergian women were hiding underneath this nervously chatting mother as she tries to tie her son closer. Heavy of experience, she gave us a Fosse interpretation as seen through a hundred-year-old tradition of psychological portraiture. Lava rose from inside her, suggesting an invisible hand, that of Bergman, watching over her.

Stefan Larsson has a fine sensitivity to the moods in Fosse's plays, as he had demonstrated before with *The Name* at the Stockholm City Theatre, but in *Dream of Autumn* he stuck to a style of acting that did not agree with the indistinct nature of the dialogue. Even the scenes with Michael Nyqvist and Marie Richardson showed obvious traces of the Dramaten tradition, though with a lighter touch than the parts of Ahlstedt and Lindblom.

Equally, the English-language theatre has obvious problems with a dramatist who gives the actors such limited chances of shining. An attempt with *Nightsongs* at the Royal Court Theatre in London was met by headshakes – this was definitely not for British theatre, which rarely deviates from the realistic and verbally equilibristic type of drama that is the strength (and weakness) of the English theatre tradition. Fosse's deep seriousness appears to be regarded by British critics and audiences as a Scandinavian speciality – gleefully referred to as 'Nordic gloom'.

With a few exceptions, the best interpretations I've seen of Fosse have been in German, four of them at Schauspielhaus in Zurich: *Nightsongs, Winter, The Son* and the monologue *The Guitar Man*. Early on, Fosse found a home here, an understanding that is partly to do with the German tradition, a curiosity versus new approaches, but also an intellectual openness that favours his dramatic writing. In Berlin, Zurich and Munich, there was a young generation of directors who had an obvious affinity with his way of writing, meaning that he does not have to answer for his lyrical dialogues or minimalist repetitions, as if he were a failed realist who needed help to turn back.

Against that background it's understandable that Thomas Ostermeier was the choice of director when *The Girl on the Sofa* had its world premiere with British actors at the 2002 Edinburgh festival. The idea of course was that a radical German director would keep the serious Norwegian playwright from falling into the Anglo-Saxon trap of psychology and realism.

This meeting of three nations had a relatively happy ending, though not without leaving a slight after-taste of compromise. The Norwegian, German and English ingredients did not quite gel, for the simple reason that the work with the structure became too apparent. What Ostermeier achieved was, for a Fosse drama, a rarely seen theatricality. The play opened in the Royal Lyceum Theatre, one of the most beautiful theatres in Edinburgh, a Victorian cream cake offering possibilities and challenges quite different from the black boxes where Fosse's shorter plays are usually performed. The effect couldn't have been more of a paradox, the actors' British idiom contrasting sharply with the iron grip of Ostermeier's Expressionist style.

In *The Girl on the Sofa*, Fosse yet again addresses the presence of time in a person's life. The girl of the title appears both as a child and as a grown woman. As a young girl, somewhere on the threshold of puberty, she witnesses a sexual act between her mother and an uncle while her father, a sailor, is absent on one of his long sailings. It leaves a deep mark on the adult woman's ability to trust in love generally and men especially. To express her feelings, she paints pictures, feeling herself that she is a failed artist. She rejects the man who wants to live with her. Left on the stage in the end are only the young girl and the adult woman, that is, the same person split into two, the one she was and the one she became.

The novelty about *The Girl on the Sofa* is the fact that Fosse here approaches psychology and offers an explanation for his main character: she became who she is due to her experience as a child. The play could be a paraphrase of Ibsen's *Little Eyolf*, which ends in a symbolic suicide – nine-year-old Eyolf, the son of Alfred and Rita Allmers, following the Rat-Wife into the sea. The other boys see Eyolf standing at the edge of the jetty and becoming "kinda dizzy" whilst staring at the Rat-Wife rowing out on the fjord. "And so it was, he fell over the edge – and was gone."

Considering Fosse's water mysticism – in *Death Variations* the daughter goes into the sea from a pier – it's not hypothetical to surmise that Ibsen's play sent him a message. At first The Daughter's line:

> I can feel your hand in my hair
> And I'm standing there at the edge

I see your hand
I see your hand
I see the dark sky
and the rain
is your hand
Pause
I want to hold your hand

Then her mother:

They found her in the morning
Floating in the sea
Brief pause
She was floating in the sea

Ibsen and Fosse both draw a parallel between life inadequacy and sexual trauma: Eyolf's parents have neglected him in a moment of passion and caused his physical disability (he can only walk with crutches). The event in *The Girl on the Sofa* may not have had such tragic consequences, but the parallel of her internal trauma is hard to overlook: the past harbours the truth about our lives. In one play after another, Fosse has described the relationship between parents and children without giving a closer explanation. Then, suddenly, he plays at being Ibsen and writes a recipe for the adult woman's neurosis. Ibsen, who was so strongly influenced by Freud.

As a matter of fact, Jon Fosse has always been interested in the great theme of psychoanalysis: sexuality. But his principle is to speak very quietly about it. Remember the man's statement in *Dream of Autumn*, where he says that, the more you talk about sex, or about God, the more you lose what you talk about, so that in the end only the talk remains. One of the most moving aspects in Thomas Ostermeier's production of *The Girl on the Sofa* was Abby Ford's diffident portrayal of the young main character's sexual awakening. In a central scene she tries on her sister's underwear and, for the first time, partakes of an adult experience. It was done without sensationalism, with guidance from the older sister, in such a normal unaffected way that the whole process revealed another aspect of Fosse's theatre: he strives to see things as they are, without adding to them. No explanation, no theory, can give a more exhaustive idea than the experience itself.

The picture I have drawn of a mystic and Gnostic needs to be complemented by a third statement: Fosse's connection with phenomenology. Without getting too immersed in the modern history of phenomenology – starting with Edmund Husserl and culminating with Maurice Merleau-Ponty – one can describe phenomenology as a striving to describe an immediate impression, what presents itself to our consciousness prior to interpretation and theory. Fosse's essays confirm that he is well versed in this theory, and the same goes for the plays' focus on phenomena such as time and space: the fact *that* his characters are there is more important than the question *why*.

Still, he is a playwright, not a philosopher, and he does not write to convince us of the value of certain theories. Strindberg is occasionally criticised by literary scholars for being 'unscientific' in his treatment of Schopenhauer and Indian philosophy. That may be so, but he used whatever found an echo in the rest of his material, and the same goes for Fosse's phenomenology: it's only of interest to us in so far as the ideas agree with his artistic aspiration.

In Fosse's world, there is no *present*. It could also be said: there is *only* the present. Each and every second is painfully present because it cannot be retained. Time splits itself into the small constituents of before and after. The same applies to the conscience or subject aware of this flow, not beyond time and space but merely an additional present split into before and after, as impossible to fixate as the previous: a process without beginning and end.

One thing that contributed to making Luk Perceval's *Dream of Autumn* in Munich so different was the experience of the microscosm. The fragmented phrases allowed for neither pause nor consideration. We looked straight into the disintegration of language and time. The unease imparted by the actors related to the passage of time: a feeling of constant loss. The drama was embedded in this phenomenon.

What I've always found attractive about Fosse's work is its resistance to being identified as theatre. From the very start, I've had difficulty fitting him into a traditional theatrical concept. Instead, my interest had to seek other directions, above all film and music. However tempting it was to connect certain themes in *The Child* to Ibsen's *Brand* and the theme of suicide in *Nightsongs* to Chekhov's *The Seagull*, it seemed more appropriate to note the many deviations making the little word 'not' so useful in describing his dramaturgy. This was not naturalism, not absurdism, not family drama, not ideological debate, not epic theatre, not 1990s irony, not new brutalism, not multimedia performance: none of these terms stuck to him. He was entirely his own man.

But I could see similarities with film directors such as Roberto Rossellini, Robert Bresson, Yasujiro Ozu, Michelangelo Antonioni and the early Milos Forman (that is, before his Hollywood period). Fosse did not write like Sarah Kane, Mark Ravenhill or Lars Norén, or like the leading German playwrights Botho Strauß, Marius von Mayenburg and Roland Schimmelpfennig; or Bernard-Marie Koltès, the French dramatist staged by the director Patrice Chéreau who, years later, discovered Jon Fosse and directed *Dream of Autumn* in Paris. At the time of writing this, Chéreau is planning the English world premiere of *I Am the Wind*, due in April 2011 at the Young Vic Theatre in London.

The connection between a certain type of film and phenomenology is well known, in particular from the French film debate of the 1950s. In a classical essay of 1952, the Catholic film critic Amédée Ayfre writes about Rossellini's *Germania, Anno Zero* of 1948: "No introspection, no inner dialogue, hardly any external one, no use of physiognomy". Ayfre dwells mainly on the portrayal of the child in the film: "One can't claim that he is a good or bad actor. He is beyond the scope of acting. In the same manner the spectator is beyond the categories of sympathy and antipathy in relation to him. This child has simply lived, simply existed in front of our eyes, and been surprised by the camera in this 'existence'…Rossellini himself does not take sides… From an existential viewpoint he portrays the mystery of existence."

The keywords in this Catholic-inspired analysis – "beyond the scope of acting" – lead us straight into Fosse's aesthetic.

Amédée Ayfre's essay *Néo-Réalisme et Phénoménologie*, published in 1952 in *Cahiers du Cinéma*, is the obvious point of reference and difficult to avoid if you want to trace the continuous presence of this phenomenology in the French cinematic art of the 1960s, such as the films by Truffaut and Chabrol, and later by Martin Scorcese, who was strongly influenced by European film (above all in his early films *Raging Bull* and *Casino*). The interest in Fosse's dramatic work varies with the cultural context, leading to a decline in Britain and a boost in Germany and France. Though slightly far-fetched, the fact that Norway happens to be the place where he emerged can be explained by a greater interest in Continental philosophy among Norwegian intellectuals, in contrast, for example, to a frostier climate in Sweden, where most forms of existentialism, phenomenology and non-analytical philosophy have been rejected. When in 1965 the Norwegian philosopher Arne Naess published a book presenting four twentieth century philosophers, including Sartre and Heidegger, this was seen as scandalous amongst Swedish philosophers. In his essays, Jon Fosse moves comfortably from Heidegger's existential philosophy to Ludwig Wittgenstein's love of Norwegian scenery: "I believe we should be forever grateful to Wittgenstein for building himself a cabin high up on a mountain slope in Skjolden overlooking a fjord and sitting there thinking and writing all alone surrounded by the everlasting mountains."

A Swedish or English Fosse – would that have been at all possible?

Most of Amédée Ayfre's statements about Bresson and Rossellini can be applied equally to Fosse, and neither can one overlook the affinity with Yasujiro Ozu, one of the great Japanese filmmakers beside Kenji Mizoguchi and Akira Kurosawa, according to many the greatest and in terms of lifestyle the most Japanese.

It may be that Fosse himself is unaware of this affinity, but there are some remarkable parallels between Ozu's later films and the suspended dramaturgy in plays like *The Name*, *A Summer's Day* and *Death Variations*. Considered one of Ozu's masterpieces, *Tokyo Monogatori* of 1953 is characteristic in its portrayal of an old couple visiting their children in Tokyo and soon finding that they are not as welcome as they thought. But this conflict is only a thin haze in a story mainly concerned with the passage of time and everyday life. There is a famous scene with the old couple sitting on a stone barrier by the sea looking out over the water, glittering in the sun.

Ozu repeated each scene so many times that the actors were exhausted, robbed of the personal aura generally regarded as the main asset of a professional actor.

Robert Bresson took a similar view of the actor's contribution. He refused to work with professional actors who 'performed' and searched for faces and bodies that were expressive without expressing themselves in the conventional sense; briefly put, they were to exist beyond the scope of acting. In a study, the film director and screenwriter Paul Schrader compares Ozu, Bresson and Carl Dreyer. Buddhism is to Ozu what Catholicism is to Bresson and Rossellini. From his direction each one of them approaches the point where, in Ayfre's words, the very mystery of existence emerges from the being itself, from what is.

An interesting method is Ozu's low positioning of the camera, putting us on a level with the characters, instilling a feeling that we see them while there is still time, before we have a chance to judge them. Hear what he has to say about one of his best films, *Akibiyori (Late Autumn)*: "I want to portray a person's character by eliminating all dramatic approaches. I want people to feel what life is without these dramatic peaks and valleys." This could have been taken out of Ayfre's programme.

Falk Richter's version of *Nightsongs* at Schauspielhaus in Zurich was a revelation. It opened in September 2000 and remained on the repertoire for several seasons, confirming the interest German-language audiences, directors and actors have in Fosse's theatre. Mainly it was of course thanks to the quality of this production: the feeling that the young couple in the play – played by Judith Engel and Sebastian Rudolph – were prisoners in a trivial drama that could not be explained by either psychology or sociology. It made us *see*, not with the support of a theory but with our own eyes.

I caught a glimpse of the kind of actor required for playing Fosse. Judith Engel's sensitivity saves her from most pitfalls of her profession. She succeeded in portraying the balance on Fosse's scales – between homelessness and presence, between anxiety and the feeling of liberation that can emerge in the middle of a vacuum. A year later I saw her as a remarkable Viola in *Twelfth Night*, directed by Christoph Marthaler – ethereal, somnambular, alienated, one single rejection of the ravishing comedic types tempted by this popular role, as if Fosse's hypnotic style of acting had merged with Shakespeare's themes of individual confusion and disintegration.

Jossi Wieler's version of *Winter* at Schauspielhaus in Zurich could have competed with Richter's *Nightsongs* in the art of letting the material speak for itself without added interpretation. Played as nakedly as this, Fosse comes as close as can be to a thriller writer on stage. Together with *Visits* and *The Son*, *Winter* belongs to what can be termed the more or less realistic period of Fosse's theatre. In *The Son*, the parents are paid an unexpected visit by a maladjusted son. What happens is that an   alcoholic asthmatic neighbour, through an accident – he is pushed – falls over on the floor and dies. Nothing changes, the son leaves, and had it not been for the echoing desolation, the result of this plot could have been termed banal. But if Fosse is drawn to the banal it's not in the sense of the indifferent. The closer he gets to the trivial, the stronger the light shines out of the darkness. He embraces trivia tenderly, comforts us with the help of empathy and recognition. We are taught to doubt – doubt the identity, our own subjectivity, the present as a fixed point of consideration, everything we believe we know. We are connected with a presence that is not secretive or, as in psychoanalysis, hiding something, only showing people contained in the world and everyday life.

When the woman in *Nightsongs* decides to break up and move in with Baste – he has come to collect her – she discovers her attachment to the things filling up the home, simple things like a vase or the contents of a drawer; clothes, kitchen utensils: the simpler they are, the harder to part from. She stays in her home, not as a riposte to Ibsen's Nora but because she realizes, and we with her, that these trivial objects are *also* her, they are already in her and she in them:

> We have
> *Nods her head backwards*
> lived together quite a long time
> he and I
> had a child together
> we did
> Yes
> You must realize
> Bought things
> together
> not a lot of things
> but some

I'm sure it would have been simpler
if we'd had many things
not just a few
a few pictures
bowls
tablecloths
a few quite simple things
are all we have
That's why

This portrayal of a crisis contains above all a philosophy of life. But just as much it's a guideline to theatre. To play Fosse you need to have the courage to be amongst these 'things'. Without prejudice.

12. EXIT

I never saw Claude Régy's production of *Someone Will Arrive* at the Théâtre des Amandiers in Nanterre in the autumn of 1999. It was soon given the distinction of being one of the boldest and most interesting Fosse performances, not only because of its length, three hours, but because it instilled in the audience a state of extreme attentiveness and nerve-racking exhaustion. However, I did see Régy's version of *Death Variations* three years later, also of considerable length, and after a mere twenty minutes found myself in a no-man's land of sleep and wake. With the actors' slow motion, and with the dialogue drawn out to a swell of consonants and vowels, the experience turned into something best described by the title of one of Régy's excellent books of ideas: *L'état d'incertitude*, the state of uncertainty.

When Axel Bogousslavsky made his first entrance playing the part of The Older Man, the tempo was so low and the light so dim, it made me doubt whether he was actually there, a shadow emerging halfway out of the set upstage left, and then slowly approaching the audience. The words assumed a life of their own when there was no longer a connection between facial expressions and gestures. The slowness broke the bonds. Playing entirely without physiognomy. Nothing could be 'read'.

In Fosse's plays, we are reminded of the human face. "I can't bear seeing your face," says the girl's father in *Death Variations*, directing the words to the mother, who tells him that she's been to the hospital and seen the girl "lying there": "no longer in her face". In *Afternoon* a similar experience occurs:

> At home
> when only you and I are there
> alone

well like now
only the two of us together
well then your face will be normal
or most often it will be normal
but as soon as we're out
it stiffens
becomes kind of beautiful

"I see straight through you", continues the man: "I don't believe in you because I don't notice your doubt". Régy suddenly made me understand how Fosse indicates a path away from the rulebook that thinks it can read a human being and, without reflection, uses the face as a key to his or her inner life: character, morals or soul. "We are not the face", says Ibsen's wife Suzannah in Fosse's play about her. The Portuguese writer Fernando Pessoa writes in his *Book of Disquiet* something that would also apply to Fosse:

> It would be better for human beings if they couldn't see their own face. It is the most terrible of all sights. Nature gave man the privilege of not having to see it, like the privilege of not having to look into his own eyes. Only in the water of rivers and lakes could he see his face. And the very position necessary to do so was symbolic. He had to bend down, lower himself to commit the shameful act of seeing himself. The creator of the mirror poisoned the human soul.

When Fosse writes about the human face, it's unconnected with the responsibility for The Other central to Emmauel Lévinas' ethic. Fosse's plays deal with moral issues only indirectly. I have read analyses connecting him with Lévinas' influential facial philosophy, but when Fosse writes about the face it's more to inspire silence, revealing how little we know about The Other. The moral sphere is not excluded from this mode of thinking but, considering Fosse's openness to the various references of religious language, it's hardly primary. I like to think that contained in this stance is a bold acting theory. He goes further and further into silence. In one of his latest plays, *I Am the Wind*, two persons are out at sea in a boat, when one of them stumbles and falls in the water. Even in one of his first lines it becomes obvious that the man is gone, that is, dead: but in Fosse's world nothing is absolute or literal, neither death nor life.

The entire play is a fantasy – perhaps above all a fantasy connected to events in the much earlier play *A Summer's Day*, where Asle takes his boat out on the fjord, leaving his wife alone at the window, waiting year in and year out for him to return. These returning suicides in Fosse's dramatic work are no physical acts. All we are told about the happenings in *I Am The Wind* is that one of the men falls or jumps into the sea. It's a poetic image of death in life and life in death; to the question why he did it, he replies:

> I was too heavy
> and the sea too light

Never has there been such a clear indication of the close bond between Fosse's dramatic writing and his poetry, which breathes in the rhythmic undulations of the dialogue, strongly seasoned by the author's New Norwegian idiom. "A human being is here/and then he's gone/in a wind/disappearing/inwards/to meet the movement of the stone" is the start of a poem in the collection *Eye in Wind* of 2003. In *I Am The Wind* the lyrical voice is stronger than in anything else he's written for the stage. It can best be described as an inner dialogue, as if the two people in the boat were the same individual, partaking in a journey back and forth over the border between life and death. "But it's terrifying", one of them says about being out at sea, in daylight and darkness. And he gets the only reasonable answer:

> Yes
> I suppose it is

SOURCES

Andersen, Hadre Oftedal *Ikkje for ingenting, Jon Fosses dramatikk* Helsinki 2004

Augustin, *Bekännelser, Skellefteå*, 1990

Banu, Georges *Le théâtre ou l'instant habité*, Paris 1993

Bresson, Robert *Notes sur la cinématographie*, Paris 1975

Didong, Paula *Incarnations des idées, Le jeu d'acteur dans le théâtre francais contemporain*, Stockholm 2003

Ehrenberg, Alain *La fatigue d'être soi, Dépression et societé*, Paris 1998

Goldman, Michael, Ibsen, *The Dramaturgy of Fear*, New York 1999

Green, André *The Dead Mother*, Edited by Gregorio Kohon, The New Library of Psychoanalysis, London 1999

Hverven, Tom Egil *Å lese etter familien, Forsok om norsk litteratur på 1900-talet*, Oslo 1999

Ibsen, Nutidsdramaer 1877-99, Oslo 1978

Jonas, Hans *Gnosis und spätantiker Geist I-II*, Göttingen 1954, *The Gnostic Religion*, Boston 2001

Meister Eckhart, *Medeltida mystik*, Skellefteå 1997, *Selected Writings*, London 1994, *Du Détachement et autres textes*, Paris 1995, *Å bli den du er. Perspektiver på menneskets frihet*, Oslo 2000

Nightingale, Benedict *The future of Theatre*, London 1998

Olsson, Anders *Läsningar av intet*, Stockholm 2000

Pessoa, Fernando, *Orons bok*, Stockholm 1991

Régy, Claude *Espaces Perdus*, Besançon 1998, *L'ordre des morts*, Besançon 1999, *L'état d'incertitude*, Besancon 2002

Roudinesco, Elisabeth *Pourquoi la psychanalyse?*, Paris 1999

Schrader, Paul *Transcendental Style in Film*, Berkeley 1972

Shakespeare, William *The Complete Works*, Oxford 1988

Sofokles, Aeschylus, *Antigone*, Greske tragediar, Oslo 1993

Strindberg, August, *Kammarspel*, Stockholm 1991

Stueland, Espen *Å ersatte lykka med ett komma*, Essay om cesur, rituell forseintkomming i produksjonen til Jon Fosse, Oslo 1996

ARTICLES

Ayfre, Amédée *Néo-Realisme et Phénoménologie*, Cahiers du Cinema 17/1952

Bjørneboe, Therese *Jon Fosse på europeiske scener*, Samtiden 1/2003, *Tre forsøk over et drømmespill*, Norsk Shakespearetidskrift 1/2002

Dag og Tid, November 22, 2003, supplement on Jon Fosse

Ring, Lars *Fosse fångar en modern samtid*, Svenska Dagbladet November 12, 2001

Periodical Peripeti 1/2004 Aarhus, special edition on the theatre of Jon Fosse

Periodical Viskningar och rop 7/1999 and 9/2000

BIBLIOGRAPHY

PROSE

Raudt, svart (Red, Black) a novel, 1983

Stengd gitar (Closed Guitar), a novel, 1985, 1993

Blod. Steinen er. (Blood. The stone is), a short story, 1987

Naustet (The Boat-Shed), a novel, 1989, 1991, 1998, 2001

Flaskesamlaren (The Bottle-Collector), a novel, 1991

Bly og vatn (Lead and Water), a novel 1992, 1993

To forteljingar (Two Stories), 1993

Prosa frå ein oppvekst (Prose of Growing Up) 1994

Melancholia I (Melancholy I), a novel, 1995, 1997, 1999

Melancholia II (Melancholy II), a novel, 1996, 1997, 1999

Eldre kortare prosa med 7 bilete av Camilla Waerenskjold (Older Short Stories with 7 pictures by Camilla Wærenskjold) 1998

Morgon og kveld (Morning and Evening), a novel, 2000,2001

Det er Ales (Aliss in The Fire), 2004, 2005

POETRY

Engel med vatn i augene (Angel with watery eyes) 1986

Hundens bevegelsar (The Dog's Movements) 1990

Hund og engel (Dog and Angel)

Dikt (Poems) 1986-1992. 1995

Nye dikt (New poems) 1997

Dikt (Poems) 1986-2000.2001

Auge i vind (Eye in The Wind) 2003

PLAYS

Og aldri ska vi skiljast (And We Shall Never Part), 1994

Nokon kjem til å komme (Someone Will Arrive), 1996, 2004

Namnet (The Name), 1995,1998

Barnet/Mor og barn/Sonen (The Child/Mother and Child/The Son), 1997

Gitarmannen (The Guitar Man), a monologue, 1997

Natta syng sine songar/Ein sommars dag (Nightsongs/A Summer's Day), 1998

Teaterstykke 1 (Plays 1), 1999

Draum om hausten (Dream of Autumn), 1999

Besok/Vinter/Ettermiddag (Visits/Winter/Afternoon), 2000

Teaterstykke 2 (Plays 2), 2001

Vakkert (Beautiful), 2001

Dodsvariationer (Death Variations), 2002

Jenta i sofaen (The Girl on The Sofa), 2003

Lilla/Suzannah (Purple/Suzannah), 2004

Dei dode hundane/Sa Ka La (The Dead Dogs/Sa Ka La), 2005

Teaterstykke 3 (Plays 3), 2005

Svevn/Varmt (Sleep/Hot) 2006

Rambuku/Skuggar (Rambuku/Shadows) 2007

Eg er vinden (I Am The Wind) 2008

Andvake (Sleepless) 2008

Teaterstykke 4 (Plays 4) 2009

Jente i gul regnjakke (The Girl in The Yellow Raincoat) 2010

PLAYS IN ENGLISH PUBLISHED BY OBERON BOOKS:

Fosse: Plays One, 2004

Fosse: Plays Two, 2005

Fosse: Plays Three, 2005

Fosse: Plays Four, 2006

Fosse: Plays Five, 2011

Fosse: Plays Six, (forthcoming in 2012)

CHILDREN'S BOOKS

Uendeleg seint (Incredibly slow) A picture book, ill. by Alf-Kåre Berg, 1989

Kant (The Edge) A picture book ill. by Roj Friberg 1990, ill. by Akin Duzakin 2005

Dyrehagen Hardanger (Hardanger Zoo) Stories for children 1993

Vått og svart (Wet and Black) A picture book ill. by Akin Duzakin, 1994

Nei å nei (No and no) A fable 1996

Du å du (You and you) A fable 1996

Fy og fy (Fie and fie) A fable 1997

Soster (Sister) Ill. by Leong Và 2000

ESSAYS

Frå telling via showing til writing (From telling via showing to writing), 1989

Gnostiske essay (Gnostic essays), 1999, 2004

WORLD PREMIERES

Og aldri ska vi skiljast (And We Shall Never Part), Den Nationale Scene, Bergen 1994

Namnet (The Name), Den Nationale Scene, Bergen 1995,

Nokon kjem til å komme (Someone Will Arrive), Det Norske Teatret, Oslo,1996

Barnet (The Child), Nationaltheateret, Oslo, 1996

Mor og barn (Mother and Child), Nationaltheateret, Oslo, 1996

Sonen (The Son), Nationaltheateret, Oslo, 1997

Natta syng sine songar (Nightsongs), Rogaland Teater, Stavanger, 1997

Gitarmannen (The Guitar Man), Cinnober Theater, Gothenburg, 1998

Ein sommars dag (A Summer's Day), Det Norske Teatret, Oslo, 1999

Draum om hausten (Dream of Autumn), Nationaltheateret, Oslo, 1999

Besok (Visits), Den Nationale Scene, 2000

Medan lyset går ned og alt blir svart (While the lights go down and all is black), Teater Ibsen, Skien, 1999

Sov du vesle barnet mitt (Sleep You Little Child of Mine) Théatre de Folle Pensée, France 2000

Vinter (Winter), Rogaland Teater, Stavanger, 2000

Ettermiddag (Afternoon), Teaterhögskolan, Stockholm, 2000

Vakkert (Beautiful), Det Norske Teatret, Oslo, 2001

Dodsvariationer (Death Variations), Nationaltheateret, Oslo, 2001

Jenta i sofaen (The Girl on The Sofa), Royal Lyceum Theatre, Edinburgh, 20022003

Lilla (Purple), Royal National Theatre, London, 2003

Suzannah (Suzannah), NRK Fjernsynet, 2004

Dei dode hundane (The Dead Dogs), Rogaland Teater, Stavanger, 2004

Sa Ka La (Sa Ka La), Aarhus Teater, 2004

Svevn (Sleep), Nationaltheateret, Oslo 2005

Varmt (Hot), Deutsches Theater, Berlin 2005

Rambuku (Rambuku), Det Norske Theatret, Oslo 2006

Skuggar (Shadows), Münchner Kammerspiele, Munich 2006

Eg er vinden (I Am The Wind), Festspilene Bergen 2007

Ylajali (Ylajali), Det Kongelige Teater, Copenhagen 2008

Andvake (Sleepless), Det Norske Theatret, Oslo 2009

Jente i gul regnjakke (The Girl in The Yellow Raincoat), Kungliga Dramatiska Teatern, Stockholm, 2009

INDEX